THE
RESUME
HANDBOOK

FIFTH EDITION

How to Write Outstanding Resumes & Cover Letters for Every Situation

Arthur D. Rosenberg

Avon, Massachusetts

DEDICATION

My friend and coauthor, Dave Hizer, is no longer able to share with us his insights and guidance. As with the previous edition, *The Resume Handbook 5th Edition* is devoted to his fond memory. Heartfelt thanks to my dear Catherine and to my publisher, Adams Media.

Copyright © 2008 by Arthur D. Rosenberg
All rights reserved.
This book, or parts thereof, may not be reproduced in any form without permission from the publisher; exceptions are made for brief excerpts used in published reviews.

Published by Adams Media, a division of F+W Media, Inc.
57 Littlefield Street
Avon, MA 02322
www.adamsmedia.com

ISBN-10: 1-59869-459-6
ISBN-13: 978-1-59869-459-8

Library of Congress Cataloging-in-Publication Data

Rosenberg, Arthur D.
The resume handbook / Arthur D. Rosenberg. — 5th ed.
p. cm.
ISBN-13: 978-1-59869-459-8 (pbk.)
ISBN-10: 1-59869-459-6 (pbk.)
1. Résumés (Employment) I. Title.
HF5383.H53 2007
650.14'2—dc22
2007016521

Printed in the United States of America.
J I H G F E D

This publication is designed to provide accurate and authoritative information with regard to the subject matter covered. It is sold with the understanding that the publisher is not engaged in rendering legal, accounting, or other professional advice. If legal advice or other expert assistance is required, the services of a competent professional person should be sought.
—From a *Declaration of Principles* jointly adopted by a Committee of the American Bar Association and a Committee of Publishers and Associations

Many of the designations used by manufacturers and sellers to distinguish their product are claimed as trademarks. Where those designations appear in this book and Adams Media was aware of a trademark claim, the designations have been printed with initial capital letters.

This book is available at quantity discounts for bulk purchases.
For information, please call 1-800-289-0963.

About the Authors

Art Rosenberg is a New York/New Jersey–based consultant specializing in business analysis, project management, and U.S. Customs Compliance. His major publications include *Career Busters: 22 Ways People Mess Up Their Careers and How to Avoid Them*, *Manipulative Memos: Control Your Career Through the Medium of the Memo*, contributed chapters to *The Requirements of Programming* and *Preparing for a Successful Interview*, *Chess for Children and the Young at Heart*, and numerous articles.

Art is a former textbook publisher, translator, and language teacher who continues to provide career-related seminars to professional and minority groups. His eclectic interests include sports, chess, wine, fine dining, travel, music, and good books.

Dave Hizer was a Detroit-based executive search consultant who dedicated his efforts to matching talented executives with his clients' organizations. He brought to his profession more than thirty years of experience in executive searches, organizational development, public speaking, human resources, and outplacement.

Dave used to read more resumes per week than the number of newspaper headlines skimmed by most people in a year. He authored countless articles on career planning, self-marketing strategies, and related topics, including "The ABC's of Cover Letters" in *National Business Employment Weekly*. He also made time to frequent conduct workshops and seminars on leadership and career/life planning.

Contents

Preface

The purpose of your resume is to obtain an interview.

A successful resume will attract an interviewer's interest in meeting you.

What, exactly, is a resume? It is a *summary* of your skills and employment background. It is not an autobiographical profile, nor is it intended to make people like you or admire you.

Think of your resume as a special tool with one specific purpose: *winning an interview.*

Bottom line: You've got to make an effort to win your interview, and only the inexperienced and naïve think otherwise. Your resume is a wedge designed to get your foot inside the doors of companies where you might like to work. Obviously, if you fail to win the interview, you're not likely to get the job.

Equally obvious, there are other resumes out there in competition with your own. So yours must be at least as good as all the others if you're to stand an even chance. If your resume is *better,* it may give you the advantage.

Writing an interview-winning resume requires an understanding of what to say, and how to say it. For this, you need *The Resume Handbook.*

Just as the purpose of your resume is to obtain the interview, the purpose of *The Resume Handbook* is to illustrate successful resume techniques.

The Resume Handbook tells you what kind of information to include in your resume and what to leave out. Then it provides you with the tools and techniques to present your chosen facts in a convincing and engaging manner.

The Resume Handbook will help you *win the interview.*

The rest is up to you!

Introduction

After reading many thousands of resumes over the years, one recurring impression looms large and dominant: An astonishing number of resumes are poorly written, and the overwhelming majority are overwhelmingly dull!

Ah, but a veritable work of "art vitae" does happen by on rare occasion, illuminated with a spark of creative thought and pleasing to the eye. If this alone is not enough to render life exciting, it may at least make your resume interesting to read, and perhaps inspire sufficient curiosity to get you invited for a closer look, which is, of course, the purpose of your resume.

To this end, the purpose of this book is to improve the quality of some of the resumes we, and others, may be called upon to read over the coming months.

We have taken care to avoid the fat and wordy formats to which some resume books are prone. Instead, we've tried to heed our own advice on writing resumes by making our book interesting and relevant. *The Resume Handbook* presents the essential ingredients that go into successful resumes, with lucid explanations and the clearest of examples.

You can read through this book in less time than it takes to write a resume, then use it as a reference source when you are ready to begin writing your very own.

You will find many examples in Chapter 4, The Best Resumes We've Ever Seen. Once you've learned what makes them so effective, you will be able to apply these winning techniques to your own purposes. Chapter 5, The Worst Resumes We've Ever Seen, illustrates some of the pitfalls to be avoided.

The Resume Handbook focuses on three major objectives:

- *Organization:* How to structure and infuse visual impact into your resume to capture the reader's attention.
- *The Basic Principles:* What to include and what to leave out of your resume, to avoid wasting the reader's time and running the risk of turning him/her off.
- *Accomplishments:* How to write action-oriented accomplishments by using action verbs, enabling you to represent yourself as a highly motivated achiever.

You'll also find sections on networking, using the Internet, cover and personal sales letters, and other helpful advice. As always, our emphasis remains on writing resumes to help you present yourself in the most appealing and engaging manner possible, to help you win the interviews you want.

A Message from the Author

Since the original edition of *The Resume Handbook* was published in 1985, more than 280,000 copies have been sold. Comments and reviews from our readers confirm that the reasons for our book's success lie in its clearly written style, direct and practical advice, and occasional touch of humor. After all, a helpful book need not be dull and lifeless, any more than a winning resume.

The job market has somewhat improved since the last edition of *The Resume Handbook*, but the competition for the best positions has, if anything, intensified. Consider this to be our offering to help you navigate the swirling clouds and currents toward positioning yourself in the direction of your choice.

Your feedback will be welcome at *art.rosenberg@att.net*.

CHAPTER ONE
Looking for a New Job

Looking for a new job? Nearly everyone does, sooner or later. The U.S. Bureau of Labor Statistics informs us that the average American worker seeks a new employer every 3.6 years; in fact, the National Bureau of Economic Research suggests that Ethan, Emily, and Angel are likely to work for ten different employers during their respective lifetimes. With job-market volatility still on the rise, we need to be ready for an accelerated rate of change.

More than 50 million Americans (out of about 140 million employed and 7 million unemployed) are currently involved in some sort of career change or transition. More than a third of these searchers are currently employed, motivated in large part by economic uncertainty, job and career dissatisfaction, fierce competition in the job market, and an increased awareness of alternative career opportunities.

These statistics are partially skewed by firms that hire nearly as many new workers in a given year as their total number of employees. For example, a construction company with 100 workers may have to hire as many as 200 per year, due to enormous turnover. And service firms with as few as twenty-five full-time employees often need to hire four times that number each year in order to maintain a stable staff.

The bottom line is that if you are looking for a job, you are in excellent company. To compete successfully, however, you need a method that will give you an advantage. This is where *The Resume Handbook* can help, because whatever job-search methods you may use, you'd better have a darned good resume to penetrate the screening processes used by most employers.

All They Know of You

The purpose of your resume is to get you invited for an interview. It precedes you in your job search like an emissary of good will, an advertisement of your skills, experience, and knowledge presented in their most favorable light. Until you meet the interviewer (if you ever do), the resume is all they know of you. Approximately one interview is granted for every 300 to 400 resumes received. Obviously, a mediocre resume will rarely win an interview; a poor one has no chance!

Research tells us that a piece of advertising matter has about a second and a half in which to attract the reader's interest. Someone sitting with a towering stack of resumes is simply unable to accord them equal time. Your objective is to position yours to receive its fair share of the interviewer's attention.

Read on . . . we'll show you how.

Who Needs a Resume?

You do, even if you're not looking for a job.

Fact: The majority of desirable positions are offered to individuals who are employed and may not even be seeking a new job. You never know when opportunity will knock, when the "job of a lifetime" may dangle within reach. Obviously, it pays to have an updated copy of your resume at hand for unexpected opportunities.

Fact: It is a valuable experience to observe your own career on paper. A well-organized resume can place your past experience, growth, and goals into perspective and help chart the path of your future career.

Fact: Having a resume may help protect you from the unexpected, like losing your job in an economic turndown. A good resume takes some of the anxiety out of the job search. This is especially true for the experienced professional who suddenly finds him- or herself competing for jobs against young professionals who may be better versed in the latest job-hunting techniques.

Resume Organization

There are three commonly used resume formats (examples in Chapter 4):

1. *Chronological* resumes are standard for people with unbroken records of employment. This straightforward, easy-to-follow format lists the dates of current and past employers.

2. *Functional* (thematic) resumes focus rather on accomplishments than dates. This format is practical for those with employment gaps due to unemployment, or other activities they might prefer not to reveal (such as jobs from which they were fired or left after a short time, unsuccessful self-employment, addiction rehabilitation, and a host of other reasons).

   It is also a better way to emphasize specific aspects of your career.

   Example: If you spent eleven years teaching engineering and only two years as an industrial engineer, a chronological resume would draw attention to your teaching background. But if you happened to be looking for an engineering position, the functional format would allow you to play up your industrial experience and de-emphasize the academic side.

Another rationale for choosing the functional approach is if you have little to list by way of experience. This tends to be the case with recent graduates and also people seeking new (or planning to resume) careers after prolonged periods at home.

3. *Combined* chronological/functional resumes can, under the right circumstances, combine the best of two worlds.

Resume Preparation

Composing an autobiographical outline requires serious thought and preparation. Find a quiet spot (office, den, or dining room table) where you feel comfortable and undisturbed. Set aside a period of four to five hours and, if possible, turn off the phone.

Collect all the materials you will need, including:

- Pens, pencils, or PC—whatever you like using best
- A lined pad (at least 8½" x 11")
- A good dictionary and a thesaurus
- Records of your past employment, education, and related materials
- Copies of former job applications and correspondence, if available
- Descriptions of some jobs for which you plan to apply
- A copy of *The Resume Handbook*

Now that you're suitably equipped, you can begin to formulate your own *resume strategy*. Be careful to observe the basic principles of resume writing, which follow next.

CHAPTER TWO
The Basics of Writing Resumes

Having a successful resume is a necessity for all career-minded people. Writing one is a cross between art and science, a balance of logic and aesthetics. The final result must look good while reflecting certain basic principles.

The suggestions offered in this and later chapters have been formulated through long years of exposure to all sorts of resumes. Major deviations from these guidelines are at your own creative—and professional—risk.

Brief Is Often Better

If you are launching your career and have limited work experience, keep your resume to a single page. Avoid unnecessary and irrelevant materials. Even experienced individuals can, and usually should, limit theirs to two pages. Bear in mind that no one wants to read long, rambling resumes, especially when they are poorly organized and overly wordy.

See Chapter 4 for more about the following exceptions:

- Specialized resumes, as in the sciences and academia, may need to reflect extensive and diverse experience, publications, and related information.
- Consulting resumes are expected to list relevant technical skills, projects, and a comprehensive list of clients.

Format

Your name (in bold type or capital letters), address, and cell/home/work telephone number(s) belong on top:

Rose Shagorofsky

275 Palisades Avenue
Bridgeport, CT 06610

bevdoc@college.com
cell (203) 650-4321

Devon H. McCormick, CFA

521 E. 14th St., #11H

New York, NY 10009

D: (212) 938-6551; E: (212) 529-2418; C: (646) 729-5817

devon@acm.org

Objective

Next comes your objective (if, in fact, you decide to include this topic) and a summary of your qualifications, accomplishments, employment history, education, and related activities and affiliations. Select the resume from the samples provided in Chapter 4 that most closely meets your needs and suits your style and use it as a model, or combine elements from several of the examples:

Objective

A paralegal position in a legal firm that includes insurance among its specialties. Seeking an opportunity to apply my experience in insurance law and expand it into other legal areas.

Only include objectives on a resume if they are clearly stated and consistent with your accomplishments and demonstrated skills. Also, be sure they address the position you are responding to. If they're looking for a lion tamer, they're not interested in reading about floral arrangements.

If you do include an objective, understand the difference between *career* and *job* objectives:

- A career objective is a long-range plan that may or may not relate directly to the job for which you are applying;
- A job objective is targeted to a specific job. To avoid confusion, consider using the term objective by itself, which would be appropriate for many situations.

There are potential dangers of stating an objective:

- Limiting your job search to a narrow or dead-end arena
- Discovering at the interview that the employer has a need that is different from the job you were considering, but is one in which you may be qualified and interested
- Confusing or turning off the reader

Avoid terms like *challenging* and *rewarding* which are self-serving and of little interest to most employers. *Their* challenge and reward is to hire employees who can help their company. In other words, hone your objectives to the job for which you are applying.

Education

Education should precede employment history only if you are a recent graduate with little or no work experience, or if you are trying to change your career and have a degree that is more closely related to the position you are seeking than your employment history.

Optional Categories

Optional categories include objectives, summary of qualifications (and similar topics), and personal details (in most cases these are best left out) such as date of birth, marital status, military record, and health.

Summary of Qualifications

A detailed resume that includes a wealth of professional experience can employ this idea effectively. The summary may be inserted in addition to, or instead of, objectives, or the two can be combined into a *qualifications and objectives* section.

Note that there are many ways to represent a summary, and other labels to identify them:

Business Experience:

Over fifteen years of administrative and sales management in finance and insurance. Consistent record of improving financial results, operational effectiveness, and customer service.

Profile:

A highly motivated and effective business analyst experienced in project management and software implementation. Specialties encompass financial, institutional, and retail applications. Proven strengths include problem solving, system specifications development, and system test coordination. Consistent record of promotions and increased responsibilities over the past thirteen years from programmer to project and business manager.

SERVICE
Team and project management; business analysis and testing; assessment and creation of innovative documentation and training materials, compliance and requirements documents, RFP's, and proposals. Applications include a wide range of financial services, pharmaceuticals, telecommunications, insurance, sales and marketing, publishing, and human resources.

A well-worded summary may entice the reader to read further or, conversely, to stop reading. It can be helpful if the applicant has had an extremely diversified background, including (for instance) teaching and industry, especially if the resume extends beyond a single page. A well-written summary attracts the reader's eye, brings the essence of your resume into focus, and compels the reader to move on to the main details.

Personal Data
Conventional and straightforward personal details may lend an air of respectability to your image, but nonessential information is more likely to work against you.

Realistically, prejudices do exist against single women, unmarried men over a certain age, and senior job seekers. Your date of birth may only serve to persuade potential employers to believe that you are too young (or old) for the job before the interviewer has even met you. Further, unless your physical or mental condition might limit your ability to perform traditional job functions, you should leave out references to health.

On the other hand, a military record may be worth mentioning if it includes specific job training or experience (such as technical or organizational).

Leave out:
- Reasons for leaving a job: They can be covered at the interview.
- Salary (past or desired): You need to know about the job in order to make sure you do not ask for too little or too much. Never risk eliminating yourself from the running before the race has started.
- Hobbies/memberships in social or religious organizations: A potential employer has no need of these details, and you cannot predict what may turn them off.
- Reasons for not having served in the military.
- Any potentially negative information about you—unless it involves

a prison term, lost lawsuits, or handicaps that may affect your job performance.

- The label "Resume" or "Vitae": If a glance fails to clearly identify your resume as such, the label will not help.

Visual Impact

Use a consistent type style throughout your resume—boldface, italics, and caps will serve for headings and emphasis. Never send photocopies; either have your resume professionally printed, or use a high-quality laser printer. The difference is well worth the cost.

Print your resume on white or off-white quality paper. Make sure the resume is *letter perfect* by having it critiqued and proofread by someone reliable. Errors, typos, stains, abbreviations (etc., e.g., i.e.), technical jargon, and hip slang or buzzwords are strictly taboo.

Ensure Integrity

Poorly conceived and written resumes tend to lack internal integrity, so make sure yours is consistent. If you include a job or career objective, support it by accomplishments. If you are interested in a high-level management position, emphasize your accomplishments in related management areas, any creative programs you may have developed, and so on.

If you include a Summary of Qualifications, assure that it briefly and truly represents the bulk of your resume. Otherwise you will alienate the reader. All the information in your resume needs to be consistent and interrelated.

Employment History

A chronological resume should strike a balance between job content and accomplishments (as you will see in the following chapter). Begin with your current position and work back chronologically. Provide more detail on recent jobs, less on those you held further back in time. Avoid verifiable exaggerations that might constitute grounds for dismissal, and remember to use action verbs and phrases to present the facts to your advantage (Chapter 3).

Here is an example of a balanced job history:

1999 to present   Flinthall Electronics, Dover, Ohio. Manager of product testing. Supervised testing group consisting of five industrial engineers whose mission was to institute methods for testing performance, job safety, and durability of projected products. While heading up this group:

- Initiated testing methods that reduced annual budget of group by 29%.
- Received award of excellence for innovations in testing by American Society of Research Engineers—2002.
- Increased group efficiency (time and quantity parameters) by 19%.
- Developed eleven patented testing procedures.

Use the opening paragraph to clarify the job's objective. This lends clarity and objectivity to the accomplishments.

Organizations to Which You Belong

It is okay to list groups that demonstrate achievement or professional standing, such as the National Association of Certified Public Accountants, or the Tool & Diemaker's Guild. You can also indicate your leadership abilities as an officer or official in a strictly uncontroversial association, like the PTA or Junior Achievement. On the other hand, stay clear of political, religious, and potentially controversial groups, which absolutely do not belong on resumes.

Awards

Do list awards that may relate to the employment you are seeking (for instance, Pulitzer Prizes, honorary doctorates, and so on). Leave out references to bowling or karate championships. Although such achievements may bolster your ego, they can create uncertain images in the mind of the interviewer. In addition, they have nothing to do with the job of winning the interview.

• • •

With these basic resume strategy guidelines in mind, we will now move on to creating a resume that will stand out from all the others.

CHAPTER THREE
Describing Your Accomplishments

The way you describe your accomplishments is at least as important as the facts you list. Active, energetic phrases attract the reader's attention—dull and passive words will put him/her to sleep.

Examples: "Created" has more impact than "began;" and "promoted," "instituted," and "produced" hold more attention than "worked on," "became," or "finished."

In fact, the first words used to describe your accomplishments can make the difference between an impressive resume and one that's just ho-hum. Which may determine if it is being read or tossed into the circular file.

With this in mind, let us pause to digest "Hizer's 57"—a list of action verbs that introduce an *action person*, the kind employers notice. Then we'll present the mechanics of how to state your accomplishments in their best possible light.

Action Verbs

HIZER'S 57

administered	directed	negotiated
advanced	eliminated	organized
advised	established	planned
analyzed	evaluated	prepared
authored	expanded	produced
automated	focused	promoted
coached	headed up	provided
conceptualized	identified	published
conducted	implemented	reduced
contained	improved	researched
contracted	increased	restructured
controlled	initiated	reversed
coordinated	innovated	saved
created	instituted	streamlined
cut	introduced	supervised
decreased	led	taught
designed	maintained	trained
developed	managed	trimmed

This may not be the ultimate list of all existing action verbs, but you can apply one or more of them to just about any field, industry, or profession in order to demonstrate why your skills would be an asset to an employer.

Now that you are equipped with these effective action verbs, let's turn them into action phrases that illustrate your accomplishments in their best light.

Action Phrases

Dull resumes tend to offer the kinds of images that look like they were copied right from corporate personnel files: little more than recycled and overused clichés. Clearly a poor resume strategy.

The Resume Handbook way is to use descriptions that stress your noteworthy accomplishments in a manner that attracts and holds the reader's attention.

An interview-winning resume balances job content with accomplishments, weaving them into an attention-getting style. Call it flair, technique, or pizzazz . . . we think of it as *impact*.

To illustrate this point, we offer several typical and contrasting examples of the kinds of statements typically found in resumes. Those on the left are dull and tell only half the story: what was done. The action phrases on the right present a larger context in which accomplishments can be evaluated in a meaningful context. These are also more interesting to read because of their effective use of action verbs.

Dull	With Impact
1. Raised sales from previous year.	1. Reversed 3-year negative sales trend; sales up 17% over prior year and 22% over past 3-year average.
2. Began new employee programs, lowering turnover.	2. Created and launched two new employee relations programs (flextime and job posting), resulting in a 19% turnover reduction.
3. Handled bookings for elderly pop group.	3. Administered bookings, travel, and accommodations for octogenarian octet.
4. Housewife for the past seven years.	4. Managed and organized six-member household with annual budget of $65,000.
5. Marketed new travel plan to corporations, increasing sales $19 million.	5. Initiated new market concept of packaging travel to corporations for incentive programs, resulting in sales of $19 million (more than double expectations).
6. Worked for losing congressional candidate for ten months.	6. Organized and coordinated political campaign for leading gubernatorial candidate.
7. Opened new sales offices in two cities that made quotas ahead of schedule.	7. Researched feasibility, then established two new sales offices; both operated above sales quotas within two years (eight months ahead of schedule).

8. Hired and trained six new polar bear tamers since 2005. Only one serious casualty.	8. Recruited, trained, and motivated six new polar bear tamers since 2005; five continue to excel.
9. Lowered operating costs in my division by $2.1 million.	9. Initiated cost reducing plan resulting in a 27% ($1,210,000) cost reduction with no negative effect on production capability.
10. Scheduled and ran software orientation classes for managers.	10. Conducted leadership training for forty-eight supervisory and management level staff members.
11. Increased sales and profitability during budget cuts.	11. Expanded profitability and market penetration sales by 14% during a period of budgetary cutbacks.
12. Contributed to efficiency of our department.	12. Increased group efficiency as measured by time and quantity parameters by 35%.
13. Wrote ornithology procedures manual for museum.	13. Conceptualized and authored eighty-eight-page ornithology procedures manual for museum zoological research department.

The above examples illustrate a relationship between action verbs and more complete and detailed descriptions of accomplishments. This is because action verbs invite further questions—even as you reflect on your personal achievements and create your own resume.

Remember to focus on meaningful accomplishments that produced a noticeable and/or measurable effect on the environment in which you worked. Refer to the following list of questions to stimulate your memory and description of what you accomplished:

1. Did you increase sales or productivity or meet/exceed goals, quotas, or expectations?
2. Did you reduce costs/losses and save money? Did you keep key accounts or clients?
3. Did you identify and resolve any major issues?
4. Did you establish any new or innovative systems or procedures? Don't forget to include meaningful timelines and cost or quality results.
5. Did you re-engineer any procedures? With what results?
6. Did you show yourself to be a team player?
7. Did you demonstrate recognized leadership skills? Briefly explain how, and what resulted.
8. Did you train colleagues or subordinates to meet or surpass expectations? What training techniques did you use?
9. Did you introduce any new services or products? What resulted?
10. Did you serve as a coordinator, liaison, representative, or committee

member in a capacity that made a difference? What difference did it make?

11. Did you demonstrate a willingness to assume additional responsibilities?
12. Did you accomplish something that was considered difficult or impossible?
13. Did you establish a record of consistency and reliability, such as completing projects on time?
14. Did you ever clean up someone else's mess?
15. Did you perform independently without close supervision? What were the results?
16. Did you go way out of your way to provide exceptional service to a client or customer? What happened as a result?
17. Was your work performance recognized by a superior? Elaborate, briefly.
18. Have you ever been told by a peer, superior, supplier, or customer that you made an important difference? What was the result?
19. What was the most unusual and professionally satisfying thing you've ever done on the job? What resulted?

A skillful blend of action verbs and meaningful accomplishments are likely to attract the interviewer's attention and, hopefully, motivate him/her to invite you for an interview.

Skim through the following examples and compare them to your own accomplishments:

- Successfully managed a four-member household with an annual budget of $64,000 while completing an Associate Business degree at Valley Community College.
- Researched, wrote, and published an information booklet for college seniors on how to manage their finances.
- Conceptualized and founded Meadow Lane Day Care Center, which now cares for thirty-three preschool children.
- Controlled expenses on "Parents March for M.S."; treasurer for Imperial and Essex Counties.
- Organized food cooperative that purchased $324,000 in consumables (2001–5).
- Created children's T-shirt design, then implemented marketing program resulting in gross sales in excess of $70,000.
- Maintained 3.9 grade-point average in business courses at Louisiana State University: completed nineteen courses to date.
- Elected to represent Indiana University at the International Congress on Energy Alternatives in Havana.
- Chosen over thirty-seven other trainees by senior management to rewrite a training program.
- Created neighborhood theater ensemble, which developed into the nationally renowned "Westgate Orchards Theatre Ensemble."
- Written up in Oregon's Eye O-U (alumni newspaper) as one of ten most promising freshmen in 2007.

- Initiated and headed ninety-member "Students for Intellectual Expansion"—University of North Dakota's answer to president's challenge to create alternative energy.
- Conducted sensitive quality control study for Southeast Michigan Water Authority—written up in Michigan Congressional Record, June 2006, "Standing Ovation for H2O."
- Formed local Junior Chamber of Commerce, which has grown to 567 members.
- Elected to Board of Directors of the $450-million asset Tri-County Employees Credit Union.
- Originated and published "Salescall," an informational newsletter distributed to over 400 sales representatives throughout the United States. "Salescall" covers sales techniques, product knowledge, legislative updates, notes of competition, and technical changes.
- Headed up procedures group that eliminated nearly forty obsolete reports and modified, or combined, over a dozen others without reducing operational effectiveness.
- Designed assembly pivot arm that increased overall line speed by 11%, resulting in an increase in daily production of thirty-nine units (15% increase).
- Produced videotape program entitled "Here to Help," outlining Marcot's product servicing capabilities to current and prospective clients.
- Instituted self-developed safety program within my production wing of 179 employees, resulting in lost workday savings of 39% over previous three years.

The above statements are action-oriented not only because they start with action verbs but also because the statements are achievement-oriented: They demonstrate the writer's abilities to organize, lead, and get things done. Check out the following examples:

Using quantitative measures to delineate the extent to which an achievement was completed.
Example: Scored in the 89th percentile on twelve out of the fourteen sections of the state-licensing exam for plumbers.

Using position to indicate the relative importance of the achievement.
Example: Awarded second place out of sixty entrants in the National Collegiate Debate Association "Debate 2007" in St. Louis.

Using action verbs to indicate selection over others.
Example: Selected fifth for the pre-supervisory awareness program at Big Sky Electric out of 195 candidates.

Using action verbs to show leadership in creating, initiating, or heading an activity.
Example: Organized and led 36-member church bazaar group that successfully raised $28,760 over a two-year period.

For Students and the Newly Graduated

A special note to students, new graduates, and those returning to work after a lengthy absence: Look outside the workplace to create your accomplishment statements. If you have limited or outdated work experience, you must select from personal experiences in order to market yourself to potential employers:

1. Describe your membership and leadership activities in campus clubs and organizations. (Leave out any controversial activities.)
   Example: "Captained coed softball team that won campus championship, 2006. Recruited, coached, and motivated eighteen players."

2. Look for an accomplishment statement in a term project or paper that you wrote. This is especially advantageous if it relates to your job objective or career interest.
   Example: "Researched and wrote twenty-one-page term paper, "Which Niche Now," listing innovative approaches in identifying and appealing to product markets. (Received an 'A.')"

3. Mold an accomplishment statement around a noteworthy comment made by a professor, instructor, or teacher that shows your creativity, insight, and hard work.
   Example: "Recognized verbally by organic chemistry professor, who stated that I had 'natural research instincts' and that I was 'bound for greater heights.'"

4. Include accomplishment statements that demonstrate initiative and responsibility.
   Example: "Initiated, organized, and led almost entire dormitory popul tion in preparing for Parents' Day—June 2007. The parents enthusiast cally praised the day's events."

5. Think in terms of specialized training and learning experiences that exhibit uniqueness or an interest in learning new things.
   Example: "Volunteered to stay after hours (without pay) to learn and work with bookkeeper to close out financial books; subsequently closed out next month's books on own—also without pay."

For Those Returning to Work After an Absence

1. Include volunteer work—school, civil, or community.
   Example: "Named 'Volunteer of the Year' by Landfill County School Board in 2006.

2. Identify how interests and hobbies suggest uniqueness or expertise.
   Example: "Featured in *Furniture Refinishing* magazine (April 2005) for volunteer work teaching high school sophomores and juniors furniture repair and refinishing."

3. Show how you have found ways to keep your skills updated.
   Example: "Established home-based research and advisory service on the Internet to provide corporate clients with current patent and copyright filings."

4. Explore how management of family functions can serve as work-relevant accomplishments.
   Example: "Conducted research leading to identification of a rare learning disorder previously undiagnosed by doctors and clinicians. This identification led to successful treatment and article in *Parents* magazine entitled 'How a Parent Made a Difference.'"

5. Consider how continuing education and self-development demonstrates your initiative and sense of responsibility.
   Example: "During 2005–2007 completed three Dale Carnegie courses on Sales, Leadership, and Public Speaking. Named top graduate in leadership program."

Describing Your Education

Limited employment experience raises the potential relevance of your educational background to the position you are seeking. In this case, education may be listed above accomplishments. Whether it is your key accomplishment or subordinate to your job history, your educational background can be presented in an impressive and appropriate manner.

If you have extensive employment experience, the bare details may be sufficient:

2007: B.S., Chemistry, Howard University, Washington, D.C.

or

Cornell University, Ithaca, N.Y.: M.B.A., International Business Administration

Feel free to include any academic honors earned:

2007: San Diego State University, San Diego, California: M.A., Sports Management (*cum laude*).

or

University of New Hampshire, 2006: B.A. in Political Sleight of Hand; graduated *summa cum laude*.

If your employment experience is limited, it may help to describe your pre-employment educational achievements:

2007—Bachelor of Arts Degree in Business Administration, University of Florida. Achieved 3.6 grade-point average (4.0 scale); specialized in Invisible Information Systems. Senior project consisted of 223-page report on the compatibility of selected information retrieval systems. Excerpts published in July 2008 edition of *M.I.S.*

or

Boston University, College of Inner-Communications, 2007. Maintained 3.5/4.0 GPA. Served as editor of *The Daily Free Press* (2004–2006) emphasizing journalism sequence; awarded Juan Scali Achievement Prize for best student investigative news story.

If you have extensive relevant work experience in an academic setting (as do researchers, law students, journalism students, and others), be sure to carefully describe your accomplishments with action phrases. Limited employment experience particularly necessitates creativity in describing other educational achievements. For example, a lecture heard at college, work, or elsewhere may be described as:

December 2001: Attended seminar on "Business Computer Languages" at RETI School of Electronics, Rapid City, SD.

or

Summer 1998: Participated in weeklong seminar on publishing procedures and marketing techniques, University of New Mexico.

List any relevant certificates you've earned:

Received "Internet Proficiency" certificate from ABC Business Institute, Phoenix, AZ: February, 2006.

or

Awarded certificate of proficiency in "Business Communications Machinery" from Control Info Institute, 2007.

If you lack a college degree, emphasize any classes attended or years completed. This can be worded so as to suggest that you may be in the process of completing a degree:

UNIVERSITY OF MIAMI (Evening Division): B.S., Athletic Sociology; in progress.

or

Currently working toward B.S. degree in Private Administration, University of Delaware.

People with extensive professional experience commonly list the seminars, lectures, or certificate programs they have attended, and so should you. Those who haven't earned college degrees are advised to list their high school diplomas. For example:

Diploma (with honors), Davis High School, Mt. Vernon, N.Y.

or

Graduated (college preparatory courses) Saltwater High School, Orlando, FL.

All They Know of You

Following these guidelines on stating your accomplishments, your resume should fairly sing to an employer: Call me in for an interview; I can help your company. Remember, your resume is all they know of you until you walk through that door. The only way an employer can identify you as an action-oriented individual is from your resume, and action verbs will help you to accomplish this objective.

Having mastered the art of using action verbs, your remaining task is largely mechanical: plugging these action phrases into the general format described on the next page.

When stating your accomplishments, be sure to include the following:

- Name and location of the organization (city/state only; street address is unnecessary)
- Specific job title
- Job description
- Skills applied
- Skills acquired (if applicable)
- Significant accomplishments
- Dates of employment (unless using functional format)

In listing former jobs, it is recommended that you go back no more than eight to ten years, unless you've spent all that time with the same company or have something significant to mention.

Gaps in employment dates of more than a month or two can be camouflaged by extending dates of earlier and later employment; an even better method is to employ a functional format. Brief explanations, such as "sabbatical to complete degree," "illness," "military service," and so on may be effective, as long as they are true and not subject to being exposed as false.

Having stated your accomplishments with action verbs and phrases that embellish your performance, you have completed the most difficult part of writing an effective resume.

Ready to begin? Before you do, first take a look at Chapters 4 and 5 to see how others have created their masterpieces . . . and disasters.

CHAPTER FOUR
The Best Resumes We've Ever Seen

The following resumes, edited and modified by the authors, are examples of the best we've ever seen. We selected them to represent the techniques and purposes we'd like to share with you.

Each resume addresses a specific challenge and approach. You may find one that appeals to you or draw on elements from two or more to meet your personal needs.

The resumes are labeled as chronological (with dates), functional (without dates), and combined (with and without dates). They are organized according to the needs and objectives of different job seekers in the following categories:

- Limited Experience
- Restaurant
- Secretarial
- Hotel Management
- Sales, Marketing, and Product Development
- Graphic Art
- Teaching
- Health Care
- Paralegal
- Human Resources
- Business Management
- Engineering
- Banking
- Finance
- Technical
- Research and Academia
- Executive
- Career Change
- Consulting

Some categories, such as Finance, Technical, Research and Consulting, may overlap. However, we have found that this organization helps our readers to find what they are looking for both easily and conveniently.

A recent graduate shows an impressive list of achievements.

Hugo Lightly   22 Story Avenue
(606) 555-1111   Lancaster, Pennsylvania 28717

—— EDUCATION ——

B.A., Penn State University, August 2006
Communications (emphasis on management), with additional major in Psychology.
Junior and Senior GPA: 3.7: Overall GPA: 3.3

—— SELECTED ACHIEVEMENTS ——

• Scored in the top three percent of all graduating college seniors in the United States on the
GMAT (Graduate Management Admissions Test) and in the top five percent on the analytical/
problem solving abilities portion of the GRE (Graduate Records Examination).
• Elected by 104 residents to position as Hall President, Hershey Residence Hall, Penn State
University, 2002–2006.
• Excellent writing ability as demonstrated by a 3.5 GPA in writing classes, 95% average on
senior-year term papers, and an entry in school creative writing annual.
• Chosen to be Research Assistant within School of Communications, Spring 2003 and as
Teaching Assistant for Summer, 2004.
• Member of Dean's List at PSU three times (3.5) GPA.
• State Finalist in Radio Broadcasting two consecutive years.
• Excellent knowledge of Microsoft software.

—— EXPERIENCE ——

Penntec Research and Development, Inc. Pittsburgh, Pennsylvania   **2005–2006**
Selected by Human Resources department manager to implement a Best Practices benchmark-
ing survey and to assist in the writing and development of a corporate-wide employee training
program for such areas as leadership, decision making, and communications. Solely responsible for the development of a 10-session leadership training program now in use throughout
Penntec's North American operations.

The DH&S Group Lancaster, Pennsylvania   **2005–Present**
Currently working as a research associate doing marketing, product, and literature research
for organizational development and team building consulting firm. Responsible for producing
literature for the group and all word-processing functions.

Kelly Temporary Services Harrisburg, Pennsylvania   **Intermittent**
Offered permanent temporary position three weeks into temporary assignment at Kelly corporate headquarters. Assisted Accounts Receivables department manager in implementation
of Total Quality Management program, and assisted Senior Account Specialist with Ford
Motor, Philip Morris, and AT&T accounts.

Straits Diving St. Ignace, Michigan   **Summers, 2004 and 2005**
Manager of a scuba diving operation with seasonal revenue of $250,000. Responsibilities in-
cluded overall management of finances, retail sales, charter operation, purchasing, community relations, and dive instruction.

Combined

A college student seeks a summer job as a nanny.

Rose Shagorofsky

275 Palisades Avenue
Bridgeport, CT 06610

bevdoc@college.edu
cell (203) 650-4321

Objective   A position as a summertime nanny for a family that values special care and education for their children. SOUNDS LIKE AN EXCELLENT OPPORTUNITY FOR A FAMILY WITH CHILDREN.

Personal   Teachers, neighbors, friends, and acquaintances know me to be a caring, level-headed, and responsible person. NICE ADDITION.

Qualifications   As a second-year biology student, I have good English, math, and science skills, as well as proper health and cleanliness standards.

Experience   Evening and weekend sleepover babysitting for three neighborhood families over a period of four years. Responsibilities included feeding and providing sanitary care for children ranging from age 2 to 7 years.

Reading to and tutoring children from preschool to second grade. Created assignments, assigned and corrected homework and summer vacation projects.

Education   **Wesleyan University**, Middletown, CT: Honors student: 3.7 (out of 4) grade average through 3 semesters. APPROPRIATE AND RELEVANT DETAILS WITHOUT A LOT OF FLUFF.
Co-chairperson, Biology Club.
Participate in inner-city tutoring program.

Bassick High School: Graduated with honors: A student.

REFERENCES ARE USUALLY ASSUMED WITHOUT THIS STATEMENT. HOWEVER, YOUNG JOB SEEKERS WITH LIMITED EXPERIENCE CAN SAFELY ADD THIS, ESPECIALLY FOR CHILD CARE WORK.

Excellent references available.

Functional

An imaginative and creative "blue-collar professional" looking for a better job.

Pierre Cuisine
MASTER CHEF

14 Boulevard Fourchette
New Orleans, Louisiana

Telephone (mornings)
(504) 555-0544

*The proper blend of training and diversified experience is my recipe for culinary excellence!
From the everyday to the extraordinary. After your clientele have tasted
my international entrees they will demand an "encore."*

CREATIVE OBJECTIVE FOR A CREATIVE BUSINESS.

EXPERIENCE

2001–Present   **Arnaud's Restaurant**   **Head Chef**
New Orleans, Louisiana

EVIDENCE OF MANAGEMENT ABILITIES AND EXPERIENCE

Manage entire kitchen staff of twenty-two that produces the finest luncheons and dinners in the South.
• Create extraordinary seafood, meat, and chicken dishes, specializing in delicate sauces.
• Supervise three assistant chefs and wine steward.
• Oversee training of four apprentices.
• Responsible for purchases of all foods and kitchen budget of $1.4 million.

1998–2001   **Le Chateau**   **Chef**
Charlesbourg, Quebec
One of two chefs directly under head chef
• Prepared special sauces and such delicate specialties as pheasant under glass.
• Served flambés and other spectacular dishes in dining room.
• Conceived and wrote all lunch menus.

1994 – 1998   **Chez Paul Beaucoup**   **Apprentice Chef**
Paris, France
• Prepared hors d'oeuvres, entrees, and desserts under the direction of one of the world's foremost chefs.
• Assisted in the purchase of foods and kitchen supplies.

EDUCATION
1994   Diploma, École d'Haute Cuisine, Lyons, France

THE TYPE OF TRAINING THAT STANDS OUT.

Generally recognized as the leading cooking school in Europe.

SPECIAL TALENTS

MAKES AN IMPORTANT POINT THAT MIGHT OTHERWISE BE OVERLOOKED.

• Capable of serving as a wine steward.
• Fluent French and English; spoken Italian and Spanish.
• Aware of kosher dietary laws.

PERSONAL

CLEVER, WITTY, APPEALING

• Dual nationality: French and Canadian.
• Willing to relocate to any civilized country.

Chronological

An administrative professional with solid office skills and a record of steady employment.

Francis L. Workday

1404 Moore Avenue
Lincoln, MO 65338

Home: (417) 555-4771
flw22@aol.com

CLEAN, DESCRIPTIVE AND HELPFUL
TO POTENTIAL EMPLOYERS.

Professional Summary

Administrative office professional with eleven years of progressively more challenging assignments. Strong computer skills in applications including word processing, spreadsheets, database, graphics, and accounting. Capable of rapidly learning new assignments involving decision making, organization of data, customer service, working cross-functionally with others and prioritizing responsibilities. Responsible and reliable; work quickly and accurately.

Technical/Office Skills

Software   Microsoft Office (Word, Excel, PowerPoint, Access); Lotus Notes.
                  Able to adapt and learn any new software.

A POSITIVE ATTITUDE IS
ALWAYS APPEALING.

Work History

A PROGRESSION OF DUTIES
AND RESPONSIBILITIES.

2003 to Present   Union Carbides; Lincoln, Nebraska
Secretary and Administrative Assistant to Vice President in Charge of Sales.
Duties include: Preparing sales reports and basic market research reports; scheduling travel arrangements for nine sales professionals; supervise two other clerical assistants; ensure that all filing, letters and reports produced by department meet quality standards for timeliness, clarity, and accuracy.

1998 to 2003   Hanson, Markham & Robb; Lincoln, Nebraska
Senior Secretary to Managing Partners of a seventeen-partner CPA firm.
Duties included: Overseeing all internal accounting for hours worked and billed. Supervising one other clerical assistant. Preparing minutes for all weekly partner meetings. Maintaining partner business development reporting and tracking. Maintaining all personnel files for firm's 29 employees. Recruiting and hiring all clerical/administrative personnel.

1996 to 1998   Second National Bank; Lincoln, Nebraska
Secretary, Commercial Loan Department
Duties included: Typing of all loan documents and departmental correspondence. Maintaining Loan Committee notes. Greeting and directing all guests.

Education and Training

Evelyn Steel Secretarial School, Lincoln, Nebraska   Received diploma and Top Student Award
for eighteen-month program. 2000
Xerox Training Center St. Louis, Missouri   Certificate of proficiency for Basic PC
training. 2000

Personal

Enjoy travel, willing to relocate.   THIS CAN'T HURT.

Chronological

A file clerk with solid office skills.

Rita L. Fantasia   ritafan@yahoo.com

1000 Minter Bridge Road   Phone: Home (503) 555-5252
Hillsboro, Oregon 97123   Office (503) 555-2525

Objective: A position as a file clerk in a progressive organization offering the possibility to advance in responsibilities.

> NOTHING WRONG WITH WANTING
> TO MOVE UP THE LADDER.

Profile: I am cooperative, energetic, and a quick learner.

Skills: Typing 70 wpm accurately; word processing; spreadsheets.

> OFFICE SKILLS THAT
> ARE IN DEMAND.

Employment

Venus Beauty Products, Portland, Oregon   January 2006–Present
Major beauty products supply distributor and retailer.
File Clerk:Maintain customer and product filing systems

McMan Law Office, LLC, Hillsboro   March 2004–January 2006
Law firm specializing in real estate and taxes.
File Clerk:Organized and maintained client and receivables filing systems

RadiSys Corporation, Hillsboro   January 1999–March 2004
Hardware/software company.
Mail/File Clerk: Sorted/distributed mail and expanded customer and product filing systems.

Education:

Currently taking courses toward an Associate Business Degree at Portland State University, School of Business Administration, Portland, Oregon. CREDIBILITY!

Diploma, Hillsboro High School.

Chronological

A hotel clerk trying to make the move into management.

Roosevelt A. Jackson

2704 W 37th Place
Chicago, IL 60632

jackson101@att.net
Home (773)-879-6817

A REASONABLE OBJECTIVE,
BACKED BY EXPERIENCE.

Objective: Having successfully worked my way from desk clerk to Assistant Manager of a landmark Chicago hotel, I am seeking an opportunity to manage the front desk operations of an upscale, mid-sized hotel.

Profile: Employers, colleagues, and hotel guests have often commented on my friendly attitude and positive results. Supervisors confirm that I am well organized and detail oriented.

Employment History

March 2004–Present   **Assistant Manager,** Holiday Inn Hotel, Chicago City Centre

- Hire and terminate employees in a department of more than 35 staff members.
- Supervise desk staff.
- Personally handle special and difficult reservations, resolve guest complaints.
- Assist in weekly labor scheduling.
- Supervise no-show billing and correspondence.

INCREASED RESPONSIBILITIES
SHOW CAREER PROGRESS.

March 2004–January 2006   **Desk Clerk,** Hotel Blake

- Handled reservations, guest check-in and out.
- Accepted and balanced cash and credit card transactions for Magnificent Mile Hotel.
- Resolved guest complaints.

March 2004–January 2006   **Desk and Housekeeping Clerk,** Days Inn Chicago

- Handled reservations, guest check-in and out.
- Prepared housekeeping inventories.
- Ensured guest room standards.
- Resolved guest complaints.

Education

Associate Degree in Hotel Management, Kennedy-King College, Chicago.
Diploma, Bowen High School, South Chicago.

Skills

Standard MicroSoft Office software.

Chronological

**An upbeat, creative presentation of
an impressive track record in big-ticket marketing.**

Merrie R. Noël
200 Nesbit Trail
Alpharetta, Georgia 30201
(404)555-0000
yuletime@atp.com

CONFIDENCE IS AN ESSENTIAL
ASSET IN SALES.

OBJECTIVE Endless horizons in marketing or sales management with a progressive, dynamic company that needs and appreciates a results-oriented and highly experienced professional.

PROFESSIONAL ACHIEVEMENTS

STRATEGIC ACCOUNT MANAGER

RESULTS THAT COUNT.

• Achieved superior track record in developing new business.
• Implemented new market strategies to establish added-value programs resulting in $17 million of new business over a two-year period.
• Researched and analyzed market trends in specific consumer and industrial market segments to ensure fitness of products for growth.

SENIOR FIELD MARKET DEVELOPMENT SPECIALIST

• Identified and developed over $10 million of new business.
• Developed successful partnerships with strategic end-user companies.
• Positioned new materials for developing applications providing manufacturing advantages to the end user.
• Integrated resources into end-user engineering and design functions to optimize material selection, performance, and design for manufacturability.
• Coordinated product, molding, and design seminars resulting in joint development programs with end-user companies.

VICE PRESIDENT

LONG- AND SHORT-TERM SUCCESS.

• Co-founded First Source Corporation, a manufacturer and distributor of specialty and proprietary chemicals for the food, pharmaceutical, and personal care industries.
• Nurtured this entrepreneurial venture from infancy into a $3 million business in thirty-six months.
• Maintained responsibility for sales, marketing, profit, and loss.

PRODUCT MANAGER, SILICONE FLUIDS

MORE SOLID RESULTS.

• Developed and implemented marketing strategies for nationally marketed silicones.
• Increased sales volume from $7 million to $12 million by second year.
• Motivated, directed, and routed activities of seven sales representatives and twenty-two distributors.
• Designed, coordinated, and implemented a professional/educational training program for corporate and distributor sales forces.

Combined

A highly experienced, versatile, professional manager who puts his best foot forward.

Christopher Athenas

42 East 73rd Avenue
Tulsa, OK 74115

E-mail: chris_lib@abc.com
Home: 405/555-0000
Office: 405/555-0001

ABILITY TO IDENTIFY, FORMULATE, and MARKET HIGH PAYOFF PROJECTS:
Developed projects that led to birth of 6,000 terminal communications network, $40 million-a-year wholesale company (the Arbor House Specials seen on TV), installing M.B.O., annual marketing plan in division of 1450, and an accounting system for bookstores.

> WELL-PHRASED HEADINGS.

ABILITY TO START, GROW, AND MANAGE DEPARTMENTS: Started and managed: 5 training departments, research department, personnel department, and district sales office. Played key role starting 70 national account sales departments and 2 research departments.

> IMPRESSIVE NUMBERS.

P&L RESPONSIBILITY: Started division with $166,500 budget; now over $4.8 million.

ABILITY TO WORK AT TOP LEVELS: Setting up board summit meetings to develop corporate objectives. Directly responsible to board for several projects. Staff person in charge of FOUR board committees. Serviced group coverage working with top management and unions.

SCOPE OF TRAINING EXPERIENCE: Managing and delivering: Sales training, management and organizational development, plus clerical and technical training. Developing, staffing, and selling 50 workshops with 5,000 enrollees per year, throughout North America.

SCOPE OF RESEARCH EXPERIENCE: Managing: Market research, new product development, operations improvement, R&D, and fact-base development and maintenance. Create and conduct census of retail flower shops, primary source of data for floral industry.

Positions:

> COMBINATION OF EXPERIENCES SHOWS BOTH VERSATILITY AND DEPTH.

2002–Present	Director, Education and Research Division. Arbor House. International association; 1200 retail bookstores.
1999–2002	Management Consultant for consulting firm of Martell and Coxwell, Inc. Worked with National Association of Healthcare Affiliates, Timon Mufflers, and Oceanic Airlines.
1997–1999	Manager, Employee Development Department, Ohio Healthcare Affiliates.
1992–1997	Manager of various sales, training, and personnel functions. Including the Automobile Club of Ohio.

> EMPHASIS ON CONTINUING EDUCATION.

Education: BA, Economics, Washington State University, Seattle, Washington
Over 1500 classroom hours at University of Tulsa.

> NOTICE THE AMOUNT OF IMPACT A ONE-PAGE RESUME CAN EVOKE!

Combined

A graphic design professional tracks his progression into management.

Michael Angelo

3000 S. Valley View Blvd.
Las Vegas, Nevada 89102

cistine@aol.com
(702) 555-9999

OBJECTIVE
Management position in visual communications where strong operations management, graphic design capacity, and ability to develop staff will contribute to the productivity and profitability of the organization.

WELL-STATED OBJECTIVE.

PROFESSIONAL SUMMARY *Versatile graphic design professional with thirty years of marketing-oriented experience including production management, two- and three-dimensional graphic problem solving, staff development, logistic sensitivity, in-depth knowledge of reproduction systems, and long-standing record in creative resolution of customer needs.*

OBJECTIVE SUMMARY BACKED BY DETAILS THAT FOLLOW.

SIGNIFICANT ACCOMPLISHMENTS
MANAGEMENT, OPERATIONS

SPECIFIC, MEASURABLE ACCOMPLISHMENTS.

• Restructured production organization of 190 employees with fifteen supervisors on three shifts to 170 employees with eleven supervisors on two shifts while accommodating 20% increase in sales and workload.
• Streamlined procedures integrating related creative functions under fewer supervisors. Created multi-skilled technicians to avoid overstaffing. Annual profit increased from $65,000 to $750,000 in two years.
• Reversed operating losses in group producing $360,000 in annual sales. Increased group sales to $1,365,000. Workforce reduced from eleven to eight; group is now a profit leader.
• Authored purchasing/receiving/inventory control program to reduce inventory on hand by 50%, to $225,000. Upgraded requisition system from numbered adhesive tags to electronic entry. Revision allowed first accurate P&L reports.

MANAGEMENT, HUMAN RESOURCES

BROKEN DOWN INTO CATEGORIES.

• Instituted revolutionary employee evaluation procedure to include employee in performance analysis, goal setting, and determination of wage adjustment. Ninety-five percent of employees rated themselves more critically (and requested smaller wage increases) than under previous system.
• Eliminated historic animosity between first- and second-shift personnel through structured team activity and promotion concept of "sixteen-hour work cycle" to replace existing attitudes of two competing shifts.
• Identified critical system failure—order writers not trained in production methods and capabilities. Over 20% of orders impossible to complete as written. Instituted scheduled training program; erroneous orders still declining.

Combined

CREATIVE PROBLEM SOLVING

• Conceived, developed, and produced photographically generated color sample booklets to resolve client frustrations when specifying photographic color from process ink samples in standard PMS color swatch books.
• Produced 12-foot-high black and white mural from vertical crop of 16mm movie frame; heavily retouched intermediate 20" x 24" print. Copy negative of retouched print produced mural in three sections through fine mezzotint screen. Mural still on display.
• Provided display text in Arabic, German, and Russian using New York-based translation services and foreign-language typesetters. Obtained necessary entry permits and approvals; produced export documents. Arranged pre-paid services.
• Produced full-color mural to be self-supporting in traveling use as backdrop for mall fashion shows. Mural in sections, plus supporting devices, fit into carrying case less than 36" x 36".

PROGRAM DESIGN

• Consulted with more than 200 varied clients in need of A/V programs of all types, sizes, and budgets. Advised appropriate use of overhead transparencies vs. 35mm, computer, or optical slices; guided style and format selection. Produced roughs or storyboards from scripts or notes.
• Restructured production system and quotation to produce environmental graphics for client hospital when original quote of $400,000 proved beyond budget tolerance. Project completed for $160,000.
• Managed graphic production of major space museum project at Jackson Community College. Schedule allowed six weeks from receipt of text, NASA transparencies, and artifacts to opening. Installation completed prior to opening.

EMPLOYMENT HISTORY

2006–Present	Wonderfully Creative	Director of Production
2000–2006	Graphic Designs, Inc.	Manager, Design and Display
1991–2000	Somewhat Creative Designs, Ltd.	Graphics Manager
		Director of Show Services
1977–1991	Detroit Edison Company	Export Manager
	Graphic Designer	Account Representative

MANAGEMENT DEVELOPMENT PROGRAMS

COMPENSATES FOR THE LACK OF A COLLEGE DEGREE.

Statistical Process Control—Oakland University
The Deming Method—George Washington University
Investment in Excellence—Pacific Institute
Effective Team Facilitation—J. Farr
American Economic System—Oakland University
Managing Stress—R. Goren
Communicating for Action—T. Stafford
Statistical Thought Process—Beta Association

EDUCATION   Advertising Design—Center for Creative Studies

Combined

A relocating elementary school teacher who cares about education.

Elizabeth English
teachme@yahoo.com

12 Arcadia Drive
El Paso, Texas 79901

THE FACT THAT SHE IS
MOVING TO ANOTHER
STATE IS EXPLAINED IN A
COVER LETTER, NOT IN
THE RESUME.

Telephone: (512) 555-6543 (Res.)
(512) 555-1111 (Bus.)

Career Objective   Seeking a career continuation as an elementary education teacher where experience, results and dedication are valued.

WHEN IT COMES TO EDUCATING
CHILDREN, CARING MATTERS.

Employment

2000 to 2007   **Tippin Elementary School**, El Paso, Texas
Faculty Member.

SOLID CREDENTIALS FOR
A YOUNG TEACHER.

- Taught 2nd and 3rd grade reading, math, social studies, arts, and music.
- Participated in selection of textbooks and learning aids.
- Planned and supervised class field trips.
- Scheduled and invited speakers and demonstrations.

1999 to 2000   **Coldwell Elementary School**, El Paso, Texas
Junior Faculty Member.
- Substituted for faculty members in 1st and 2nd grade reading, math, and music.
- Attended and co-supervised class field trips.

1999 to 2000   **Coldwell Elementary School**, El Paso, Texas
Student Teacher.
- Observed classes in elementary reading, math, social studies, arts, and music.
- As Student Teacher, taught 1st grade classes under supervision of department chairperson and faculty members.

Education   George Mason University, Fairfax, VA.
Bachelor of Arts in Elementary Education, 1999.
Achieved a 4.8 GPA out of a possible 5.0.

AS A TEACHER, SHE IS PROUD
OF HER GOOD GRADES.

Chronological

A young nurse seeking to work her way up the health-care ladder.

Maricel Quigaman

4111 W Belmont Ave, Chicago, IL 60657   773-348-9999

> THIS RESUME IS SHORT
> AND TO THE POINT.

Objective: A nursing position in a major hospital.

Qualifications: Over five years experience in medical/health care.

- Broad-based knowledge of all aspects of nursing.   GOOD PRELUDE.
- Calm under pressure; cooperative, flexible team player.
- Bilingual: English and Filipino; fluent Spanish.

Experience:

> LOCAL TRACK RECORD MAKES IT
> EASY TO VERIFY REFERENCES.

2005–Present   University of Chicago Physicians Group, Chicago   <u>Nursing Aide</u>

- Provided nursing care to adults and children.
- Assisted in patient care, including counseling patients and families on health issues.

2002–2005   Friend Family Health Center, West, Chicago   <u>Nursing Intern</u>

- Provided nursing care to adults and children.   ADMIRABLE AMBITION.

Education: Currently taking preparatory courses for RN program at the University of Chicago Medical College. Nursing Diploma, College of Nursing, Manila, Philippines High School Diploma, De La Salle Santiago Zobel School, Muntinlupa City, Philippines

Chronological

A health-care professional demonstrates her skills and versatility.

Robin Jection

RJCARE@apple.com

1 Maywood Road

Roanoke, VA 24014

Residence: (804) 555-0001

Business: (804) 555-1000

EXPERIENCE

> DEMONSTRATES ORIENTATION AND
> VALUE OF MANAGEMENT ACTION.

2005 to
Present

MEDICAL CARE ASSOCIATES   Asheville, North Carolina

GENERAL MANAGER

Directly responsible for all operations of a Medicare-certified home health-care agency with annual revenue of $6,200,000. Major services include home health care, private duty care, and supplemental staffing. Nine hundred full- and part-time employees; five branch offices.

- Reorganized internal operations, resulting in monthly savings of $16,000.
- Implemented marketing programs and internal controls that resulted in 20% increase in sales.
- Managed successful transition from franchise operation to corporate branch.
- Directed implementation of computerized client and employee information system.

2001 to
2005

WALTER A. CUMMINS HOSPITAL SYSTEM   Mobile, Alabama

DIRECTOR OF MANAGEMENT SERVICES - November 2003 to October 2005

BEAUMONT SHARED SERVICES, INC.

Managed several major components of $30,000,000 per year for-profit subsidiary of hospital. Responsibilities included contract management, management consulting, strategic planning, business development, and home health care.

- Planned and implemented establishment of durable medical equipment subsidiary; generated over $400,000 in revenue. $40,000 in profit during first year.
- Initiated first comprehensive strategic planning process for Cummins Shared Services. QUANTIFIABLE RESULTS.
- Expanded contract management to include four hospitals and various consulting projects; generated revenue in excess of $200,000 per year.
- Designed comprehensive wage and benefit program for Shared Services employees; reduced personnel expenses by 15%, but maintained current staffing levels.
- Invited to speak as guest lecturer for Alabama Hospital Association on hospitals and home health care.

Chronological

Robin Jection Page 2

ASSISTANT DIRECTOR   *March 1995 to October 2003*
Complete administrative responsibility for patient support departments of 950-bed teaching hospital. Responsible for 520 employees and annual budget of $6,600,000.

- Planned and helped initiate conversion of former school into comprehensive outpatient health center.
- Organized and conducted major consulting projects in Nigeria and Saudi Arabia.
- Initiated the planning process required to streamline functions of patient service departments.

1991 to   ***ARKANSAS COMMUNITY HOSPITAL***   Little Rock, Arkansas
1995   *ADMINISTRATOR*
Full responsibility for twenty-five-bed acute care hospital with annual budget of $2,500,000.

March 1989 to ***NORTH VIRGINIA HOSPITAL SYSTEM***   Arlington, Virginia
March 1991   *ADMINISTRATIVE ASSOCIATE*   *1991*
Responsible for management functions of Clinical Pathology Department, which employed 250. Areas of responsibility included: fiscal management, laboratory and employee representation to administration, operational policies and procedures.

PERSONNEL ASSISTANT   *November 1989 to January 1991*
Responsible for provision of personnel services to all areas of hospital. Developed department's data processing systems. Administered wage and salary and grievance programs.

MILITARY   **U.S. ARMY**   *November 1982 to November 1985*
SERVICE: Stationed at Pentagon. Honorable discharge.

EDUCATION:

M.B.A.	Howard University	1989	Hospital Administration
M.A.	Jackson State	1987	Guidance and Counseling
B.S.	Morgan State	1982	Economics & Business Administration

AFFILIATIONS: *AMERICAN COLLEGE OF HOSPITAL ADMINISTRATORS (member)*

Chronological

A health-care professional with hands-on technical skills and extensive experience.

Mary Salvas-Mladek, CRA, CST, COA
6 Westcliff Drive   home: 516 473-9584
Mt. Sinai, NY 11766   work: 516 444-4099

PROFESSIONAL ACCOMPLISHMENTS   IN THIS PROFESSION, EDUCATION IS AN ON-GOING REQUIREMENT.

Department of Ophthalmology, SUNY at Stony Brook   Stony Brook, New York
Outpatient Clinic Supervisor   1990–Present
Supervise five technicians and five administrative staff in daily support of seven staff ophthalmologists and two residents. Maintain regular personal contact with area ophthalmologists to facilitate appropriate service referrals.
Senior Retinal Photographer and Ophthalmic Technician   1984–1990
Retina Consultants of Michigan   Southfield, Michigan
Senior Retinal Photographer, First Surgical Assistant, Ophthalmic Technician
1983–1984
Obertynski Eye Care Center   Dearborn, Michigan
Retinal Photographer, First Surgical Assistant, Ophthalmic Assistant   1983–1984
Arnold Turtz, MD, Lawrence Yannuzzi, MD, Yale Fisher, MD   New York, NY
Ophthalmic Technician   1976–1977
Johns Hopkins Hospital - Wilmer Institute   Baltimore, Maryland
Ophthalmic Technician   1972–1974

EDUCATION
[Maintain minimum of twenty-five continuing education credits annually.]

Marygrove College   Detroit, Michigan
National Certification as Surgical Technologist.
Eastern Connecticut State University   Willimantic, Connecticut
BA, History and Secondary Education.
Woodstock Academy   Woodstock, Connecticut
Academic Diploma.

RELATED PROFESSIONAL ACTIVITIES   DIRECTLY RELEVANT TO HER PROFESSION.
Certified Retinal Angiographer; Certified Technologist; Certified Ophthalmic Assistant
Member, Ophthalmic Photographer Society since 1978 [Vice President, L.I. Chapter O.P.S.]
Member, Association of Surgical Technologists since 1979 [past Chapter President]
Member, Joint Commission Allied Health Personnel in Ophthalmology since 1977

Chronological

A legal assistant promotes his paralegal insurance background.

Bentley P. Gosling

1919 Omro Road
Oshkosh WI 54903

Home: (920) 236-5000
parabpg@aol.com

Objective

A paralegal position in a legal firm that includes insurance among its specialties. Seeking an opportunity to apply my experience in insurance law and expand it into other legal areas.

`COMBINING EXPERIENCE AND AMBITION.`

Technical/Office Skills

Office Skills   PC literacy includes standard Microsoft Office software.
                       Willing and able to learn any new software.
                       Type 55 wpm.

`DISPLAYS A WILLINGNESS TO PERFORM ORDINARY OFFICE TASKS.`

Professional Experience

2004 to Present   **Dumskey Diddle & Doodle, Madison, WI   Legal Assistant**
                       • Provide paralegal services to attorneys in insurance settlements throughout the state of Wisconsin.

`COMPREHENSIVE AND ESSENTIAL FUNCTIONS.`

                       • Monitor transactions from start to final settlement statement: order and review claims, research background, schedule against deadlines.
                       • Assure preparation and availability of all required documents.

`ADDITIONAL RESPONSIBILITIES WITH EACH NEW JOB.`

                       • Determine outstanding liabilities.
                       • Serve as liaison for clients, insurance companies, and attorney; schedule meetings/telephone conferences; assemble required documents.
                       • Coordinate, distribute, and file all settlement documentation.

2001 to 2004   **Corbis Insurance Agency, Madison, WI   Subrogation Clerk**
                       • Reviewed and summarized medical records.
                       • Negotiated Third Party Liability cases with attorneys.
                       • Provided subscriber information to clients; assisted in completion of questionnaires.
                       • Reviewed claims, made payments for patients whose claims were approved.

1999 to 2001   **Office of the City Attorney, Oshkosh, WI   Senior Clerk**
                       Reviewed legal claims by municipal employees, prioritized cases for legal staff.

Education

University of Wisconsin-Madison   Certificate in Paralegal Studies. Introduction to Paralegal, American Legal System, Criminal Law, Litigation, Utilization of Legal Materials, and Insurance Law.

`APPROPRIATE EDUCATIONAL PREREQUISITES.`

West Bend Insurance, Madison   Insurance courses in legal and contractual terminology.

Chronological

A personnel manager looking for room to grow.

Jamal L. Kincaid

620 Meadow Ridge Drive
Birmingham, Alabama 35242

(205) 279-1234
kincaid@earthlink.com

Objective THIS IS A CLEAR OBJECTIVE.

An opportunity to lead the human resources department of a major corporation in Alabama or a neighboring state.

Experience A BRIEF AND HARD-HITTING SUMMAHY.

Over nine years of human resources management and administration. Documented record of improving employee relations and operational effectiveness while enforcing company and government requirements.

PERSONNEL BOARD OF JEFFERSON COUNTY, BIRMINGHAM *DEPUTY DIRECTOR, HUMAN SERVICES*
For the past three years I have administered the engineering and information technology sections of the civil service Merit System employee services.
- Apply state and county regulations to labor terms and conditions.
- Develop and apply human resources goals and objectives.
- Manage a significant portion of human resources budget.
- Direct employment and recruitment activities in engineering and information technology.
- Manage worker benefits and compensation.
- Compile statistics for government reports and statements.

SOUTHTRUST CORPORATION, BIRMINGHAM *HUMAN SERVICES MANAGER*
Acquired by WACHOVIA CORPORATION in November, 2004
For four years I managed the human resources department of a major financial corporation.
- Verified application of regulatory specifications to employment practices and procedures.
- Initiated affirmative action program.
- Compiled policies and procedures manual for Human Resources Department.
- Created advertising campaign for recruitment program.
- Developed and packaged new employee orientation.
- Assisted in development and scheduling of training programs.

CABLEVISION, BIRMINGHAM *ASSISTANT PERSONNEL MANAGER*
For two years I managed the acquisition and termination of over 100 service employees.
- Hired and terminated staff.
- Administered salary negotiations.
- Reduced turnover by 37%.

THOROUGH AND SUCCINCT. INCREASED RESPONSIBILITIES LEND CREDIBILITY TO HIS STATED OBJECTIVE.

Education
Bachelor of Arts Degree in Business Administration, with a minor in Employee Relations—Birmingham Southern College.

Functional

A middle-level manager with business and project management skills.

Albert A. Torre
63 Venus Lane
Staten Island, N.Y. 10314

E-Mail: atorre@si.rr.com
Business: 212-778-7657
Residence: 718-494-7518

Profile: A highly motivated and effective business analyst experienced in project management and software implementation. Specialties encompass financial, institutional, and retail applications. Proven strengths include problem solving, system specifications development, and system test coordination. Consistent record of promotions and increased responsibilities over the past thirteen years from programmer to project and business manager.

> A CLEAR AND INVITING
> SUMMARY OF EXPERIENCE AND
> ACCOMPLISHMENTS.

Professional Experience:

Prudential Securities, Incorporated (PSI)
Assistant Vice President, Branch Automation   *2001–Present*
• Serve as facilitator between business units and systems areas to define and document project requirements.
• Develop business specifications and provide programmers with requirements for technical specifications.
• Create test plans and condition catalogs.
• Conduct user training and systems demonstrations.

> GROWTH AND RECOGNITION
> WITH THE SAME EMPLOYER

Project Lead, Securities Over The Wire System (SOW)   *1999–2001*
• Developed design for new system to allow branch office users to ship and track clients' physical securities being sent to the home office for re-registration, liquidation, redemption, and related processes.
• Designed new GUI screens to replace existing CICS display utilizing Visual Basic and HTML.
• Implemented Branch to Home Office mainframe interface to replace Teletype functionality.
• Developed automated Document Requirement function, which performs a systematic notification to a branch of required documents for executing a SOW without home office consultation.

Senior Analyst, Average Price System &
Trade Allocation and Correction System   *1996–1999*
• Collaborated with senior management to prioritize all Quality Assurance issues to satisfy user requirements and ensure timely software releases of new applications.
• Trained users on system functionality and coordinated test plan execution for Securities Database.
• Assisted developers with bug fixes, user testing, and acceptance testing.
• Reduced manual workload by 35% by automating Broker Order Entry and Correction systems.

Resume Example #16: Business Management
**A middle-level manager with business and
project management skills (Continued).**

Albert A. Torre
_____

Project Lead, Standing Instruction Database System (SID)   *1995–1996*
•   Developed new system to automate the linking of PSI's institutional accounts to
the Depository Trust Company's (DTC's) database. This enabled Standing Instruction
additions, deletions, and updates to be applied systematically.
•   Collaborated with users to create an interface to systematically retrieve Standing
Instructions from DTC and store them on PSI's database each time a new institutional
account is created.

Supervisor / Systems Analyst, Corporate Securities Systems Group   *1992–1995*
•   Designed and implemented new Fraud Detection System to detect unusual client and
employee activity which was being conducted for illegal or improper purposes.
•   Developed Early Detection System to monitor debit card activity for Visa cards
issued to PSI's COMMAND clients and alert investigators of potential fraudulent Visa
activity.

Programmer, OCR / Data Entry Department   *1989–1991*
•   Coded new applications for the Optical Character Recognition (OCR) System. This
enabled handwritten new account documents to be read automatically by the system,
eliminating the manual data-entry process.
•   Designed New Accounts documents to be used within the OCR system.

Software skills: Microsoft Office, Microsoft Project, Visio, working knowledge
                          of DB2, COBOL, and HTML

Education: B.B.A., Management Information Systems, Pace University,
                          New York, NY, 1989

> APPROPRIATE SKILL-SETS AND
> ACADEMIC CREDENTIALS ROUND
> OUT THE PICTURE.

Chronological

Julio Iglesias Garcia

1001 ASUNCION
SAN JUAN, PR 00920

TEL.: 807/555-2333
HOLA@PRI.COM

Employment

2005 to PRESENT   **Carib Electro Corporation,** San Juan—Service and Quality Control Manager. Responsible for field and customer service activities along with quality control inspection of equipment to ensure compliance with customer, OSHA, and JIC standards. Additional responsibilities include purchasing and technical service manual writing. ATTENTION: PROSPECTIVE EMPLOYERS.

• Organized six-person service department to perform SAE certification testing verification of systems, resulting in 60% increase in contract revenues, along with warranty and non-warranty repairs leading to a 45% increase in repeat sales.
• Wrote technical operation and maintenance manuals for all systems manufactured.
• Reduced purchasing costs by 32% by developing and utilizing purchasing program for TRS80 computer. BOTTOM-LINE ORIENTED.

1998 to 2005   **ABZ Corporation, Xeroradiography Division**—Technical Specialist. Responsible for field service and support of all technical representatives and contractors within designated region.

• Promoted from technical representative in Ponce branch to specialist within nine months of employment; became responsible for San Juan territory.
• Reduced nationwide service call rate by developing and implementing various in-field system retrofits. GETS RESULTS.
• Relocated to develop new area in Denver-based territory, resulting in area sales increase of thirty-five systems the following year. DRAWS OUT BUSINESS AND HUMAN BEHAVIOR CLASSES.

Education   New York University, November 1998—Bachelor of Applied Science, Electronic Engineering Technology. Graduated with 3.95/4.0 GPA; primary concentrations in business communication, personnel administration, human resource management, business law, principles of marketing, and behavioral psychology.

RETS Electronic,   June 1989—Associate's Degree in Electronic Engineering Technology. Second Class FCC Radio Telephone license.

Activities   Participating member of Society of Technical Communication (STC).

Special Skills   Bilingual (English/Spanish) ESSENTIAL FOR THIS LOCATION.

Chronological

A bank teller looking for a career path.

Barney O'Doole

2600 Frederick Avenue   Home: (410) 945-1234
Baltimore, MD 21223   flw101@aol.com

Qualifications   STANDARD TELLER SKILLS PLUS INITIATIVE.

Skilled in execution of banking processes and procedures, including customer
service, sales of bank products, and daily transaction reconciliation. Experienced in
correspondence, materials management, filing systems maintenance, and data entry.

Objective   PLACING OBJECTIVE AFTER QUALIFICATIONS LENDS CREDIBILITY TO CAREER AMBITIONS.

Skilled in execution of banking processes and procedures, including customer
service, sales of bank products and daily transaction reconciliation. Experienced in
correspondence, materials management, and filing.

Technical/Office Skills: Microsoft Office (Word, Excel, PowerPoint, Access)

Work History

Bank Teller   Baltimore Union Bank, Baltimore, MD   2003–Present
- Process account transactions, deposit and reconcile daily funds.
- Introduce bank customers to new and existing bank products.
- Provide account status information.
- Execute signature functions.
- Provide input for system enhancements.
- Refer customers to designated staff

Office Assistant   Grunt, Grin and Bear, Princess Ann, MD   2001–2003
- Collected, sorted and distributed incoming mail; processed
outgoing mail.
- Promoted to Office Manager after 16 months.

ON-THE-JOB PROMOTIONS STAND OUT.

Office Assistant   Geneva College, Annapolis, MD   2000–2001
Worked afternoons and weekends at information desk to help pay
for college.   WILLINGNESS TO WORK WHILE IN COLLEGE SHOWS A POSITIVE ATTITUDE.

Education
Associate Degree, Business Management, Geneva College, Annapolis, MD 2001

Chronological

A mid-level manager looking to make a substantial jump in responsibility.

Eric von Hohauser

79 Brampton Street
Bismarck, North Dakota 58010

Res. 701/555-1001
vonman@northern.com

Business Experience:

More than fifteen years of administrative and sales management in finance and insurance. Consistent record of improving financial results, operational effectiveness, and customer service. HIGHLIGHTS SALES AND PRODUCT MANAGEMENT CAPABILITIES.

As *Financial Services Manager* for LIFE ENHANCE INSURANCE COMPANY, maintain responsibility on a national basis for new account installations, new business development, and marketing of financial products. Conduct seminar presentations to potential customer groups on a variety of financial topics relating to our product capabilities. Lead project and marketed microcomputer system installed in over 300 credit unions. Designed and implemented IRA product sold to over 100 credit unions in first six months. 2002–Current

At LAUREL SCHOOLS CREDIT UNION, Operations Officer in charge of internal operations of $22 million financial institution with 33 employees. As *Chief Operating Officer*, personally administered all lending activities, accounting, staff training, loan delinquencies, and workflow scheduling. Implemented revolving credit loan system. Designed marketing promotions and services that resulted in assets increasing from $10 million to $22 million in two years. 1999 2002

At MANUFACTURERS BANK, originated and underwrote short-term commercial construction loans; supervised $22 million portfolio. Designed operating procedures for branch office and main office departments. Developed procedures for implementation of Master Charge system, conducted training sessions with more than 300 branch personnel. Conducted analysis resulting in purchase and installation of such equipment as high-speed check photographing machines, branch camera equipment, and teller machines. 1993–1999 SHOWS ABILITY TO LEARN AND GROW.

As *Management Trainee* at HAYDEN & RUIZ, quickly looped through all sales, administration, and operations groups in 18 months, subsequently selected to fill new operations position identifying and enacting all workflow opportunities. Significantly impacted speed of customer service, quality of information/data available to staff, and decisions enabling reduction of operating expenses. 1990–1993.

EACH OF THE ABOVE PARAGRAPHS ILLUSTRATES A COMPLEMENTARY SET OF SKILLS THAT HIGHLIGHTS ERIC'S VERSATILITY.

Education:
BBA—University of Miami, Business Administration.

Community Activities:
Chairman, Administrative committee for St. Michael's Parish.
Member, Citizens Advisory Group for Board of Education.

Functional

A recent college graduate who makes an excellent representation of her brief but relevant work experience.

Heavenly Meadows

147 Deerwood Lane   (309) 555-0001
Cedar Rapids, IA 52404   hevmed@yahoo.com

Objective | THIS TYPE OF OBJECTIVE IS OKAY FOR A RECENT GRADUATE. |

A position in financial administration, financial analysis, financial planning, or funds management that will require my best efforts.

Education

BA, Financial Administration, June 2006
Iowa State University - GPA: 3.5/4.0

Employment Experience | WELL-WRITTEN STATEMENTS DEMONSTRATING A BROAD RANGE OF EXPERIENCE. |

Summers 2004 and 2005: Holt Corp., Alpha Insulation Division, Iowa City.
• Financial Analyst: Analyzed operating, pricing, and purchasing variances weekly. Prepared financial performance reports. Provided financial analysis for special projects. Took part in year-end closing and LIFO cost calculations.
• Inventory Control: Planned and conducted verification systems for the Direct Sales Force to report status of inventories accurately. Audited and reconciled inventories of the vans, mini-warehouses, and regional warehouses. Recommended methods to reduce inventory shrinkage.
• Credit Analyst: Responsible for USA Direct Sell operations. Approved or rejected sales orders from customers. Reviewed and revised customer credit limits. Wrote 80-page procedure manual for the Credit Department to help establish a consistent credit policy. Negotiated special rates with the collection agencies.

Positions Held While Attending College | CLEVER AND CREATIVE HEADING. |

2003–2006 (part-time): Iowa State University Library
Student Assistant: Duties included processing journals, checking out assigned reading and general books, door checking, and shelving books.

2006 (Summer): March Companies, Inc. Iowa City
Route Driver: Vacation relief driver; also filled in for terminated salespeople. Responsibilities included selling, delivering, accounting, banking, inventory control, and customer services.

2005 (summer): Karmond Lumber Co., Cedar Rapids
Customer Service: Assisted customers in filling their orders, trained new employees, stocked merchandise, took inventories, and made deliveries to customers' homes.

Honors and Activities | MAKING THE MOST OF LIMITED EXPERIENCE. |

Dean's Honor List—Seven terms
Volunteer Income Tax Assistance
Iowa State Finance Club Membership Director

Combined

An experienced financial professional whose extensive skills and experience justify a third page.

JOHN C. WISSE
MBA, CPA, CMA, CFM
80 Potomac Drive, Basking Ridge, NJ 07920
Home: (908) 604-6108
Mobile: (908) 410-2638

Senior Financial Executive

Results-oriented senior financial professional with expertise in financial operations, planning, reporting, auditing, start-up ventures, and implementing financial systems. Demonstrated strengths in understanding, communicating, and applying user and client requirements. Strong skills in building and maintaining teams, motivating staff, and training. Experience in energy, telecommunications, and a host of manufacturing industries. Expertise in:

THIS NO-NONSENSE SUMMARY IS BACKED UP BY THE SUPPORTING DETAILS TO FOLLOW.

- Financial Reporting, Planning, and Budgeting
- Financial/Business Case Modeling
- Statutory Accounting
- Development and Implementation of Systems
- Accounting Policies and Procedures
- GAAP and FASB Standards
- SAP, Oracle, and ADAYTUM Software
- Strategic Planning
- Business Partner Support
- Business Restructuring
- Start-up Ventures
- Process Redesigns and Business Controls
- Project Accounting and Management
- Sarbanes-Oxley
- Auditing
- International Business

AN EASY-TO-READ DISPLAY OF FINANCIAL APPLICATIONS.

Professional Experience

1999–Present: Public Service Enterprise Group, Inc. (PSEG), Newark, NJ
2001–Present: Business Planning Manager, Corporate Planning, PSEG Services Corporation
Develop and manage process to develop annual SAP budget for PSEG, a publicly traded diversified energy company with annual revenues of more than $10 billion. Support oversight of capital budget process, including review of financial projections and investment requests for new projects. Direct responsibility for:

- Directing process improvement initiatives and planning enhancements resulting in:
  - reduced budget process cycle time (a full month)
  - improved budgeting accuracy
  - removal of over ten internal audit process comments.

SUB-BULLETS HELP TO KEEP DETAILS IN PROPER CONTEXT.

An experienced financial professional whose extensive skills and experience justify a third page. (continued)

John Wisse   Page 2

- Developing and implementing process improvements for SAP FERC Module, used to prepare a general ledger in regulatory account format to meet Federal Energy Regulatory Commission compliance reporting requirements.
- Establishing written budgeting guidelines, policies, and detailed planning procedures for SAP, including written procedures to address all facets of budget creation in the SAP Controlling Module.
- Implementing a new process to record and track approved capital projects.
- Streamlining and revising management reporting, project tracking, and analysis.
- Improving internal controls to support Sarbanes-Oxley compliance.

1999–2001: Business Planning Manager, Commercial Operations Group
Directed business planning, budgeting, reporting, and financial management for PSEG Services Corporation. Provided financial and business management support for Human Resources, Accounting, Treasury, Law, Corporate Communications, and Internal Audit.

- Developed new management reporting process after formation of PSEG Services Corporation; implemented monthly financial review process for Corporation leadership teams.
- Collaborated with associates from CAP Gemini Ernst & Young to implement a new management model for Corporation's shared services. Developed and implemented SAP cost accounting processes and procedures for service level budgeting, reporting, and client billing to support a new consultancy management model.

1999: Becton, Dickinson and Company, Franklin Lakes, NJ
Assistant Controller (Interim Assignment), North American Financial Shared Services

- Managed fixed assets, accounts payable, purchasing card, and other general accounting functions for medical technology manufacturer and seller with worldwide annual revenues in excess of $3 billion.
- Coordinated Y2K implementation plan for North American Financial Shared Services organization. Participated in implementation of SAP at headquarters and remote manufacturing locations.

1986–1998: AT&T, Basking Ridge, NJ
1995–1998: Manager, Financial Reporting, Business Markets Division
Managed service level profitability reporting for major division of AT&T, with worldwide annual revenues in excess of $22 billion.

- Managed development of business plans for large Business Market Division organizations; implemented monthly reporting, budgeting, analysis, and outlook process.
- Coordinated requirements development and system test plans for implementation of new Oracle financial systems to support service level profitability reporting. Key participant in organizational restructuring activities undertaken by financial management team.
- Supported re-engineering of decision support financial systems and processes.

An experienced financial professional whose extensive skills and experience justify a third page. (continued)

John Wisse   Page 3

1994–1995 Manager, Global Business Communications Services CFO

• Directed planning and reporting functions for International business unit with revenues in excess of $3 billion. Presented monthly financial results, outlooks, and business plans to leadership team.

• Provided consultation to operational management on strategic and operational issues, corporate and business unit financial strategy, budgeting and management control, and financial and managerial accounting.

1989–1994: Accounting Manager, Controller's Organization

Served as Assistant Controller for major AT&T business unit. Managed relationships with internal and external auditors, corporate accounting, corporate tax, and business unit finance organizations.

• Implemented controllership processes for monthly close; developed balance sheet and cash flow analysis and reporting to support business unit level Economic Value Added (EVA) measurements.

• Prepared information and analysis for quarterly SEC filings; managed consolidation process and accounting for equity investments, subsidiaries, and transactions with other affiliated companies.

Education & Certifications

• Fairleigh Dickinson University, Graduate School of Business, M.B.A.—Finance, GPA 3.7
• William Paterson University, B.S.—Accounting, *Cum Laude*
• Certified Public Accountant—State of New Jersey
• Certified Management Accountant
• Certified in Financial Management

> EXPERIENCE AND QUALIFICATIONS LIKE THESE NEED NOT BE CONDENSED INTO A SHORTER RESUME.

Professional Affiliations

• American Institute of Certified Public Accountants
• New Jersey Society of Certified Public Accountants
• Institute of Management Accountants

Achievements

Martial Arts—Third-Degree Black Belt, Tae Kwon Do

Foreign Languages

Mandarin Chinese (conversational)

Chronological

An impressive array of technical skills and business applications.

Devon H. McCormick, CFA
521 E. 14th St., #11H
New York, NY 10009
(212) 529-2418; (646) 729-5817
devon@acm.org

Experience
Bank of New York—Project Manager/Business Analyst September 2006 to Present
Managed development of portfolio attribution and reporting software for asset management group.

NY Life Investment Management—Portfolio Manager/Researcher   May 2001 to June 2006
Quantitative research, factor model development, portfolio management for international equity/asset allocation portfolios.

- Managed asset allocation (fund of funds) portfolios with asset inflows over $500 million;
- Managed $360 million 4-star asset-allocation fund of domestic fixed-income and equities and international equities;
- Collaborated with research group to develop asset allocation strategies and performance monitoring;
- Wrote regular market commentary for several asset allocation funds;
- Researched, developed, and implemented dynamic linear factor model for international industry-group rotation strategy;
- Managed $25 million publicly traded EAFE mutual fund;
- Developed trade calculator to translate Industry-group rotation forecasts into specific equity trades;
- Organized and oversaw regular research meetings on international and domestic equity strategies;
- Contributed to hedge fund strategies, both existing and proposed.

USE OF BULLETS MAKES VAST LISTS OF ACCOMPLISHMENTS EASIER TO READ.

Daedalus Strategies—Researcher   March 2000 to May 2001
Research and development of forecasting systems for investing in wide variety of assets based on economically important factors; using dynamic linear models and other advanced techniques in statistics and finance.

- Invested in equity options, based on quantitative screening, to hedge long market exposure;
- Developed HTML-based equity recommendations for biotech investments (using ad-hoc quantitative analytics to help determine best values and recommended asset weightings);
- Publicity chair for international conference on array-programming languages.

An impressive array of technical skills and business applications.
(continued)

Devon H. McCormick   **Page 2**

Bankers Trust/Deutsche Bank—<u>Vice President</u>   November 1996 to March 2000
Designed, maintained, and enhanced quantitative Bayesian dynamic linear models to
forecast stock, bond, and currency returns and variances for 11 countries.

- Elicited client constraints from investment contracts to mean-variance optimize
  portfolio allocations;
- Calculated trades for futures, options, and physicals based on target allocations
  and existing portfolios;
- Analyzed economic factors, attributed performance, explained model recommendations;
- Established and maintained production databases with trade, position, pricing,
  and economic data;
- Analyzed risk and provided portfolio recommendations; evaluated risk methodologies;
- Led data warehouse project to provide real-time economic, finance, and trade
  data for research group.

Smith Barney—<u>Assistant Vice President</u>   June 1992 to November 1996
Analyzed, designed, and coded trading and position management systems for Global
Risk Management and Mortgage Backed Securities areas. Responsible for:

- Front-end trading systems;
- Position and risk management for mortgage products, including: pass-throughs,
  ARMs, CMOs, derivatives;
- Assisted traders to specify systems requirements, explain and evangelize system,
  track and troubleshoot day-to-day problems;
- Wrote and maintained rate-of-return calculator, OAS model, prepayment model,
  core analytical library for mortgage-backed research group;
- Designed, developed, and deployed information system to branch offices worldwide;
- Led project to process millions of monthly records in mortgage-backed tapes in
  order to calculate prepayments before they are available on Bloomberg;
- Architected back office position load with error reporting and recovery;
- Established coding standards;
- Designed development environment for testing, quality assurance, and production
  rollover.

ISS/Futrak (MYCA)—<u>Senior Programmer/Analyst</u>   July 1991 to April 1992
Debugged, maintained, and developed financial package for risk management, concentrating on yield-curve products.

- Troubleshot problems with customers in trading rooms and over the phone;
- Wrote modules for foreign exchange and for pricing various financial instruments
  including bonds, swaps, and option-based instruments;

An impressive array of technical skills and business applications.
(continued)

Devon H. McCormick   **Page 3**

- Set up code control and maintenance system;
- Analyzed, planned, and implemented relational database conversion from proprietary data format.

Daedalus Systems—Independent Consultant   August 1989 to July 1991
For Mobil Research, Citibank, General Electric, and a small software firm, converted risk management system from single-user to multi-user for use on network:

- Debugged, enhanced, and verified engineering system for pressure vessel design to comply with ASME specs; analyze CICS to TSO conversion;
- Upgraded management reporting system;
- Trained and educated PC users.

> WHEN YOU GO BACK BEYOND FIFTEEN TO TWENTY YEARS, SUMMARIES MAY BE SUFFICIENT.

Hardware/Software/Languages
PCs running NT, Linux, Windows, and DOS; Unix workstations; IBM mainframes. Barra, Datastream, Factset; XP, NT, Unix, Windows, DOS, MVS; Oracle, Sybase, MS-Access; Excel, emacs, HTML, LaTex, JCL, Motif, X-Windows, SCCS. APL, C, C++, emacs-lisp, Java, Javascript, perl, Matlab, S-Plus, SAS, SQL, ksh, DOS batch, BAL, BASIC, COBOL, FORTRAN, VB, VBA.

Education
B.A. in philosophy from Vassar College, 1981. Holder of CFA charter.

Related Experience and Skills
- Presented papers on Bayesian Financial Dynamic Linear models and general Baysian techniques applied to Global Industry rotation at conference and to local quant group.
- Developed curriculum, organized and taught classes on Unix, coding, and development standards.
- Publicity chair for international conference held in New York. Chairman and chief organizer of two professional development seminars; provided electronic publicity for other seminars.
- Held officer positions in local computer group: chairman and newsletter editor. Panelist at international conference.
- Member, Association for Investment Management and Research, NY Society of Security Analysts, Society of Quantitative Analysts, ACM, IEEE, SIAM, SIGAPL.
- Read and speak French and Spanish.

> A WEALTH OF SKILLS AND RELEVANT "EXTRAS."

Chronological

A research scientist with a vast educational background and an array of applied technical skills.

Prasad N. Golla

2601 Parkhaven Court, Plano, Texas 75075   Home: (972) 312 9054 Office: (972) 477 2490

Employment Experience

> A 2-PAGE RESUME WITH 2 ADDITIONAL PAGES OF ATTACHMENTS.

1998 – Present   Alcatel, Plano, Texas

Research Scientist in Alcatel's Research and Innovation Department. Currently research issues concerning next-generation telecommunications:

> HERE'S HOW TO FIT A LOT OF INFORMATION INTO A SMALL SPACE.

Switch Scheduling Algorithms	Optical Communications
Telecommunications Diagnostic Tools	Network Processors
Telecommunications Software	Availability and Reliability of Software
Telecommunications System Architecture	Routing and Border Control Protocols
Strategic Projects and Products	Real-Time Software Support

1993–1998   Southern Methodist University, Dallas, TX

Research Assistant: Covered areas of multithreading architectures, operating systems, parallel processing, and data-flow architectures. Designed a novel single processor multithreaded architecture called the Kernel-User Multithreaded Architecture (KUMA). Built tools to test, validate, verify, and obtain performance results relating to KUMA in the areas of Cache Memory Bandwidth, Branch Prediction, and Dynamic Scheduling. Simulators for KUMA were built using Verilog HDL, C and C++ Programming Languages.

1995–1997   Southern Methodist University, Dallas, TX

Instructor, Information Technology and Computers: Taught IT and computer technology to students from a wide range of disciplines, including lab work relating to Windows 95, Windows NT, various production suits, Visual Basic and Internet.

1991–1997   Southern Methodist University, Dallas, TX

Teaching Assistant, Graduate and Undergraduate Courses:

- VLSI Systems and Design: Assisted students with CAD tools such as SPICE, MAGIC.
- Microprocessor systems and Interfacing: building PC interface boards and cards using ORCAD, ALTERA tools.
- VERILOG HDL, VHDL, PAL programmers.
- Operating System Design: software projects in C and C++ programming languages.
- Parallel Processing: also called Advanced Computer Architecture.
- Structured Assembly Language Programming: Taught programming labs primarily targeted toward x86 architecture.
- Numerical Analysis: Provided assistance to Engineering and Mathematics students programming in C and FORTRAN.
- Digital Electronic Circuits Design: Assigned lab projects, served as lab instructor.

> PEOPLE WITH ADVANCED DEGREES TYPICALLY GARNER EXTENSIVE TEACHING EXPERIENCE ALONG THE WAY.

A research scientist with a vast educational background and an array of applied technical skills.

1990–1991   Hindustan Cables Limited, Hyderabad, India
Intern Assistant to Scientists at Research & Development Department.
Developed RS232C interface Fiber Optic Modem with two other teammates as a Senior Design Project. Project fulfilled part of the requirements for degree of Bachelor of Technology in Electronics and Communications Engineering.

Education

> WITH THIS MANY DEGREES, WE CAN LIGHTEN UP ON THE SUPPORTING DETAILS.

Currently pursuing Masters of Business Administration, University of Texas at Dallas
Doctor of Philosophy, Computer Engineering, Southern Methodist University
Master of Science, Computer Science, Southern Methodist University
Master of Science, Electrical Engineering, Southern Methodist University
Bachelor of Technology, Electronics and Communications Engineering, Jawaharlal Nehru Technological University, Hyderabad, India
Awarded Outstanding Graduate Student (1998), CSE Dept., School of Engineering and Applied Science, Southern Methodist University.

Professional Affiliations
Member (1993–Present), Institute of Electrical and Electronics Engineers (IEEE) and Computer Society of IEEE.

Leadership

> THIS IS AN OPTIONAL CATEGORY BUT PERMISSIBLE FOR SOMEONE WITH RELATIVELY LIMITED COMMERCIAL EMPLOYMENT EXPERIENCE.

Vice President (2005–2006), Alcatel Leadership Association (ALA), Local Chapter of National Management Association.
President, Treasurer and Sergeant of Arms (2003–2006), Alcatel Toastmasters Club.
President, Engineering Class, College of Engineering, Jawaharlal Nehru Technological University.
President (1996), Institute of Electrical and Electronic Engineers (IEEE), Southern Methodist University.
Treasurer (1994), Institute of Electrical and Electronics Engineers (IEEE), Southern Methodist University.

> WHAT BETTER WAY TO INCLUDE SO MANY POTENTIALLY RELEVANT KEY WORDS WITHOUT TAKING UP TWICE THE SPACE?

Technical Background
Thread Libraries (POSIX, SOLARIS, etc.) for Network programming (TCP/IP, UDP/IP etc) and building simulators (C++ Sim, etc.). Expert level programming skills with C, C++, Java, Pascal, Fortran, Basic languages (including Assembly Language). Visual Basic, Visual C++, Borland C++, TCL/TK, Perl, various scripting languages and shell programming. SQL and DBMS. Description languages (e.g., Verilog HDL and VHDL). Extensive logic modeling simulation background using CAD/CAE tools (e.g., SPICE, MAGIC, WorkView, AutoCAD). Digital, Analog, and Mixed ASIC Design. Altera tools for FPGA programming. Platforms include DOS, Windows, Windows 95, Windows NT, Unix (e.g., Ultrix, Sun OS, BSD, Linux), and Apple Macintosh. Thorough knowledge and vast hands-on experience with computer and network hardware (Network Administration).

A research scientist with a vast educational background and an array of applied technical skills.

Technical Publications

PUBLICATIONS ARE A NECESSARY REALITY FOR SCIENTISTS.

"Iterative scheduling algorithms for optical packet switches," J. Blanton et al., ICC Workshop, ICC 2001, Helsinki, Finland, June 2001.

"Improved Iterative Ping Pong Scheduling Algorithm for Fast Switches," Opticomm, Denver Colarado, 2001.

"Iterative scheduling algorithms for optical packet switches," John Blanton, Hal Badt, Member, IEEE, Gerard Damm, Prasad Golla, Member, IEEE, Research and Innovation Center, Alcatel USA, Richardson, Texas, to be sent to IEEE Communications Letters.

"Hardware and timing constraints for high-speed scheduler algorithms for core routers," Prasad Golla, John Blanton, Gérard Damm, to be sent to for Journal Publication.

"Impact of Polarized Traffic on Scheduling Algorithms for High Speed Optical Switches," ITCom 2001 Denver (CO), USA, Aug. 2001.

"Performance Comparison of High Speed Iterative Scheduler Algorithms," submitted to GlobeComm 2001, San Antonio (TX), USA, Nov. 2001.

"Multi-server Scheduling Algorithms for High Speed Packet Switches," Proceedings of BAS 2001 (Turkey), sponsored by Alcatel.

"Fast scheduler solutions to the problem of priorities for polarized data traffic," Gérard Damm, John Blanton, Prasad Golla, Dominique Verchère, and Mei Yang, Proceeding of IST 2001, Tehran, September 2001.

"KUMA: A Kernel-User Multithreaded Architectural Model," Prasad Golla and Eric Lin, Technical Report: 97-CSE-22, Computer Science and Engineering Department, Southern Methodist University, Dallas, TX 75275.

"Cache Memory Requirements for Multithreaded Uniprocessor Architecture," Prasad Golla and Eric Lin, Technical Report: 98-CSE-03, Computer Science and Engineering Department, Southern Methodist University, Dallas, TX 75275.

"An Extension to Tomasulo's Algorithm for Exploiting Instruction and Thread Level Parallelism in Multithreaded Processors," Prasad N. Golla and Eric C. Lin, Technical Report: 98-CSE-08, Computer Science and Engineering Department, Southern Methodist University, Dallas TX 75275.

"Limitation of branch predictors: A case for Multithreaded Architectures," Prasad N. Golla and Eric C. Lin, "Proceedings of IEEE SOUTHEASTCON," Orlando, Florida, pp. 138–143, April 1998.

"A comparison of the effect of Branch Prediction on Multithreaded and Scalar Architectures," Prasad N. Golla and Eric C. Lin, Computer Architecture News, ACM, August 1998.

"A Dynamic Scheduling Logic for Exploiting Multiple Functional Units in Single Chip Multithreaded Architectures," Prasad N. Golla and Eric C. Lin, Proceedings of the 1999 ACM Symposium on Applied Computing, San Antonio, Feb 99, pp. 466–473.

A research scientist with a vast educational background and an array of applied technical skills.

Technical Publications

"A Single-Chip Multithreaded Processor Architecture for Exploiting Instruction and Thread Level Parallelism," Prasad N Golla and Eric C Lin, Australasian Computer Architecture Conference, ACAC '99, University of Auckland, Auckland, New Zealand, 18th–20th, January, 1999.

"KUMA: A Kernel-User Multithreaded Architectural Model," Doctor of Philosophy Thesis Publication. Prasad Golla, Computer Science and Engineering Department, Southern Methodist University, Dallas, TX 75275.

Alcatel Patents (in process)
(Not updated)
US patent awarded: 1
Have a few European Patents
Number of US Patents pending.

"Fast Scheduling Algorithms for High Speed Switches and Routers involving Multiple Servers and Data Encapsulation," Provisional patent application filed on 2/17/01 (Could be filed as 6 different patents).

"QoS Enabled Scheduling Algorithms for Next Generation Internet High Capacity Core Routers," Awaiting Alcatel Patent Committee approval.

"Fast and Fair Weighted Priority assignment using Binary Tree Arbiter (Ping pong)," Awaiting Alcatel Patent Committee approval.

"Multi-level embedded Binary Tree Arbiters for handling priority parameters fast and fairly," Will be filed for approval for September 2001 Alcatel Patent Committee Meeting.

"p – persistent Binary Tree Arbiter," Will be filed for approval for September 2001 Alcatel Patent Committee Meeting.

"Shuffling Scheme to make Binary Tree Arbiter more fair,"   Will be filed for approval for September 2001 Alcatel Patent Committee Meeting.

"Two Hardware Schemes to Make Binary Tree Arbiter More Fair, Alcatel Patent Committee Meeting," Will be filed for approval for September 2001.

"A fast memory technique to handle cell aggregation for Burst Packet Composition in Optical Routers," Will be filed for approval for September 2001 Alcatel Patent Committee Meeting.

"Use of look-up based approach for fast arbitration," Will be filed for approval for September 2001 Alcatel Patent Committee Meeting.

Chronological

Roger Northman

14 McCaul Street
Toronto, Ontario MST 1WI

Home (416) 555-1514
RMNorth@aei.ca

Professional Experience

2001–Present **PUBLISHERS ASSOCIATED SERVICES, INC., Toronto, Ontario**
President and Principal: Promote and furnish cost-efficient micro-computer systems to publishing companies. Assist in selection of appropriate hardware and software designed to save time and control costs. Increase editorial and marketing productivity.

> HE SAYS A LOT WITH A FEW WELL-CHOSEN WORDS.

1997–2001 **THOMAS PUBLICATIONS, Toronto, Ontario**
President and CEO: Chief executive in charge of operations for a leading vocational/technical textbook publisher. Exercised P&L authority for all phases of management, including editorial, production, and marketing, with seventy employees reporting.

> WHEN YOU HAVE ACCOMPLISHED THIS MUCH, DETAILS CAN BE SAFELY SUMMARIZED.

Executive Vice-President: Reporting to the Chairman of the Board Administered daily operations of Mardel Publishers in Albany, NY. Position combined general management authority with supervision of marketing and sales staff. Established computerized sales information systems, resulting in better allocation of sales territories and improvements in capital investment in publishing projects.

Director, Marketing and Sales: Directed all marketing activities, including advertising, direct mail promotion, product releases, exhibits, and field selling. Developed computer database of mailing list, and organized sales communication system for timely reportage by field sales representatives.

1994–1997 **O'BRIEN-HULL BOOK COMPANY OF CANADA, Toronto, Ontario**
Held key positions in marketing and sales administration with three textbook divisions: Goutt, Collegiate Community, and Vocational/Technical. Achievements include development of first integrated product information system for college and technical/vocational ties. Introduced Professional Selling Skills program to college travelers; designed and published *Technical Education News* quarterly magazine; instrumental in converting catalogs to computer database for electronic typesetting.

Education

1994—M.B.A., University of Toronto Graduate School of Business Administration
1992—B.A., McGill University, Montreal

Chronological

Successes highlighted in the international arena.

Constance Worldly

1696 SOUTH FOURTH STREET
PHILADELPHIA, PENNSYLVANIA 19147

RESIDENCE: (215) 321-2121
MYWORLD@WORLDNET.COM

FOR A HIGHLY EXPERIENCED EXECUTIVE, A SUMMARY IS MORE CONVINCING THAN AN OBJECTIVE.

Summary

Resourceful, results-oriented executive accustomed to profit-and-loss responsibilities seeks domestic or international marketing position, preferably in high-tech materials manufacturing.

Background

A COMPREHENSIVE SYNOPSIS.

Extensive experience principally at executive level in international and domestic marketing, manufacturing, and engineering research and development, for $800 million manufacturer of precision specialty metal products. Strengths in development of production facilities and licensees in Europe and the Far East. Distinguished record in new product development and patents. Solid background in managing start-up and ongoing production operations.

ACTION PHRASES SUPPORT OBJECTIVE AND SUMMARY.

Career History

MONOLITHIC INDUSTRIES, Philadelphia, Pennsylvania   1997–PRESENT
Vice President, International Operations: 2003–PRESENT
Direct overseas marketing and licensees in Europe and Asia for manufacturer of bearings and friction materials. Annual revenue from licensees average $26 million.

• Instructed Japanese licensee on bearing manufacturing processes including powder-making, strip sintering, and related operations. Increased license fees by 315%.
• Designed and arranged financing for $26 million bearings manufacturing plant in India, generating a $5.5 million profit on $19 million in equipment sales.
• Researched market, established process, and designed manufacturing facility for low-cost production of cam bushings in Mainland China for $37 million worldwide market.

GENERAL MANAGER, BEARINGS DIVISION: 2000–2003   MEASURABLE RESULTS.
Profit and loss responsibility for all operations, including manufacturing, quality, engineering, finance, personnel, and marketing. Annual sales $60 million. Staff of 800 in four facilities.

• Restructured division on a product-line basis generating an additional 8% gross margin, reducing inventory $3 million, and increasing profits by $2.5 million from a loss position in first year of operation.
• Directed start-up of production at 100,000 square foot manufacturing plant.
• Increased market share to 60% at three major automobile companies in a declining market.

Chronological

Constance Worldy   **Page 2**

DIRECTOR OF SALES AND MARKETING: 1997–2000
Directed marketing program for OEM bearings and transmission parts. Annual sales: $75 million.
• Organized and staffed complete marketing activity. Sales growth compounded at 17% per year ($10 to $40 million) in nine years; non-automotive sales increased 300%.
• Established European licensees resulting in a $9.5 million equipment order in Rumania, licensees in France and Germany, plus new major customer accounts.

DIRECTOR OF RESEARCH AND DEVELOPMENT: 1992—1997 | PROGRESSION OF RESPONSIBILITIES. |
Directed materials research, process development, and customer engineering activities.
• Developed unique asbestos-free, paper-based friction materials generating $15 million sales (60% gross profit).
• Analyzed process for sintering of copper-lead on steel strip yielding a 300% increase in output and 40% cost reduction for an $11 million annual savings.

ALLOYS, INCORPORATED; Jennings, Iowa | SHOWS SOLID TECHNICAL BACKGROUND. | 1980–1992
RESEARCH METALLURGIST
Studied wear and fatigue properties of metals. Developed new materials involving the sintering and casting of non-ferrous metals.

EDUCATION
University of Nebraska—B.S., Physics and Mathematics
Advanced Management Training courses on Manufacturing Strategy at Harvard University Business School and at Iowa State University Graduate School of Sales and Marketing.

| THIS INVITES A PROSPECTIVE EMPLOYER TO ASK ABOUT THE DETAILS IN AN INTERVIEW. |

PATENTS AND PUBLICATIONS
Twenty-one patents dealing with materials and processes.
Numerous articles in a variety of technical and marketing publications.

ASSOCIATIONS
Society of Automotive Engineers - American Society for Metals.

Career-Changing Resumes

There are different reasons for wanting to make a career change, but the most typical include these:

- Making the transition from technical work into management
- Switching from consulting into full-time employment (or vice-versa)
- Transposing a military background, household responsibilities, or perhaps a troubled past into a brighter future; looking for part-time consulting work

Whatever your reason for wanting to pursue a new job or career path, your resume can help to redirect your skills and working history in the direction you have chosen.

Resumes 26a and b: A technical specialist with years of financial experience reorients his resume to emphasize his managerial and supervisory experience.

Resume 27: An administrator emphasizes her sales-oriented skills.

Resume 28: A clever resume can translate homemaking responsibilities into job-related skills.

Resume 29: Military experience can often be leveraged into employment in both the public and private sectors.

Resume 30: Retiring police officers and fire fighters are often in demand in a wide range of security, insurance, and investigative roles.

Resume 31: Even prison work can lead the way to gainful employment.

Resume 32: It is not unusual to find managers with consulting backgrounds.

Octavio de Diego

426 Cardinal Lane
Bedminster, NJ 07921
odediego@yahoo.com

Home: 908-781-2482
Office: 201-352-0602
Mobile: 908-342-6666

TECHNICAL SKILLS

> EVEN A SOLID TECHNICAL RESUME DOES NOT
> PROMOTE A MANAGEMENT OBJECTIVE.

Platforms: WINDOWS, UNIX.
Software: MS-Project, MS-Access, MS-Excel, MS-Word, SQL, Unix scripting.

PROFESSIONAL EXPERIENCE

2006–Present   **UBS Global Wealth Management US – Associate Director (Divisional Vice President), Information Services**

• Currently head a team of four developers to consolidate an existing report-generation process from multiple applications into a central reporting tool. Maintain and support a portfolio performance calculation system.
• Recently directed the successful assimilation of 300,000 newly acquired accounts into the performance calculation process.

2002–2005   **UBS Financial Services - Associate Vice President, Information Services**

> IMPRESSIVE TECHNICAL ACHIEVEMENTS.

• Implemented a portfolio performance calculation engine enabling the generation of portfolio performance returns for all accounts throughout the firm.
• Implemented reconciliation systems allowing performance analysts to review and reconcile 4,000 accounts within 3 days.
• Designed and developed applications resulting in availability of month-end performance results for publication within 3 days of processing.
• Met with business partners to assess strategic direction and long term goals.
• Achieved a 99% production stability record by anticipating potential problems and implementing solutions.
• Maintained productive relationships with support groups including system engineers, database administrators, change management, and quality assurance.

| 2000–2001 | **UBS | PaineWebber – Associate Manager, Information Services** |

A STEADY TRACK
RECORD OF
PROMOTIONS.

• Defined objectives, established priorities, and generated requirements for tools to satisfy Financial Advisors' and end clients' reporting needs.
• Managed the design, development, and implementation of Web based reporting applications that provided Financial Advisors and end clients with timely business-critical information.
• Established methods and procedures that resulted in stable, reliable applications with 99% uptime.
• Managed all aspects of application maintenance and support.
• Generated application documentation that significantly reduced learning curves for new developers and users.
• Achieved high levels of support by establishing and maintaining productive relationships with service providers.
• Defined objectives, established priorities, and generated requirements for a presentation builder application to provide content for and standardize the generation of Financial Advisors' presentations to clients.
• Lead the design and development of said presentation builder application.

| 1998–2000 | **EDS – Senior Project Manager, Consumer Network Financial Services Group** |

• Managed the development of Web-based report rendering and repository applications.
• Implemented Web-based report repository in various banks and financial institutions.
• Conducted formal training for internal and external users in both English and Spanish.
• Matrix-managed up to six programmers.

| 1988–1998 | **Prudential Insurance Company of America** |

Prudential Preferred Financial Services – Project Leader/Senior Business Analyst, 1994–1998
• Led team of programmers charged with developing Windows based applications providing financial and business management solutions to the company's Financial Advisors.
• Managed the implementation of a vendor-based, online testing application. This implementation, used by more than 4,000 advisors in 150 offices nationwide, won the 1996 ASTD Blue Ribbon award in the Technology Based Performance Support category.

• Responsibilities included gathering business requirements; system analysis, design and prototyping; generating technical specification; project planning and management; managing quality assurance testing; application implementation; authoring user documentation; providing user training.

• Served as key member of corporate re-engineering team. Responsible for optimizing work process flows, creating job aids and training programs for field management personnel.

• Chosen by my peers for the role of team editor. As such, assured accuracy and readability of most documentation generated by the team.

Prudential Capital Management Group - Business Analyst, 1990–1994

• Designed, developed, and implemented enhancements to Portfolio Management system handling over $12 billion in assets using RAMIS and SPX.

• Managed two programmers.

Prudential Group Operations - Programmer Analyst, 1988–1990

• Designed and developed applications to support an insurance administration and claims processing system using COBOL, CICS, and VSAM in MVS environment.

• Managed one programmer.

EDUCATION

1993–1995	Rutgers University, New Jersey
	Thirty credits toward Master's Degree in Business Administration.
1983–1987	Arcadia University, Pennsylvania
	Bachelor of Science Degree in Computer Science.
	Minors in Business Administration and Mathematics.
	Fluent in Spanish, knowledge of French.

Chronological

Octavio de Diego

426 Cardinal Lane
Bedminster, NJ 07921
Mobile: 908-342-6666

THE SAME STORY CAN BE TOLD WITH A
SLIGHTLY DIFFERENT EMPHASIS.

Home: 908-781-2482
Office: 201-352-0602
odediego@yahoo.com

SUMMARY   An understanding of the underlying reason for complex user requirements is essential to the effective development of financial and related applications. Hands-on technical skills and the ability to direct designers and developers toward a common goal are the prerequisites of a successful manager within a business environment.

Rising through the technical ranks, I have successfully managed and contributed to the design and development of a host of performance analysis, calculation, report generation, and related processes and systems throughout the Wealth Management department of a major investment institution. Steady promotions and increased responsibilities reflect a recognition of the marriage of essential technical and managerial skills.

PROFESSIONAL EXPERIENCE   THIS SETS THE TONE TOWARD MANAGEMENT.

2006–Present   **UBS Global Wealth Management US – Associate Director (Divisional Vice President), Information Services**

A MANAGEMENT-
ORIENTED DESCRIPTION
FOLLOWED BY
SUPPORTING EVIDENCE.

Currently manage a team of four technical staff members in developing strategies to consolidate an existing report-generation process from multiple applications into a central reporting tool.

• Maintain and support a portfolio performance calculation system.
• Guided and directed the successful assimilation of 300,000 newly acquired accounts into the performance calculation process.

2002–2005   **UBS Financial Services - Associate Vice President, Information Services**

THIS OPENING
STATEMENT PLACES
THE FOLLOWING
BULLETED ITEMS IN A
MANAGERIAL CONTEXT.

Managed and contributed to the design and implementation of several portfolio performance and reconciliation systems that induced the generation of new revenue and the increase of assets under management.

• Piloted the implementation of a portfolio performance calculation engine enabling the generation of portfolio performance returns for all accounts throughout the firm.
• Implemented reconciliation systems allowing performance analysts to review and reconcile 4,000 accounts within 3 days.
• Spearheaded the design and development of applications resulting in availability of month-end performance results for publication within 3 days of processing.
• Provided strategic direction and long-term goals through close cooperation with business partners.
• Achieved and maintained an excellent production stability record by anticipating potential problems and implementing solutions.

• Maintained productive relationships with support groups including system engineers, database administrators, change management, and quality assurance, which contributed greatly to the above achievements.

2001-2001

UBS | PaineWebber – Associate Manager, Information Services
Established procedures and directed both internal and Web-based reporting applications during the UBS acquisition of Paine Webber.

• Defined objectives, established priorities, and generated requirements for tools to satisfy Financial Advisors' and end clients' reporting needs.
• Managed the design, development, and implementation of Web based reporting applications to provide Financial Advisors and clients with timely business-critical information.
• Established methods and procedures resulting in stable, reliable applications with 99% uptime.
• Managed all aspects of application maintenance and support, including monitoring application usage and measuring system performance.
• Generated application documentation that significantly reduced learning curves for new developers and users.
• Achieved high levels of support by establishing and maintaining productive relationships with service providers.
• Defined objectives, established priorities, and generated requirements for a Presentation Builder application to provide content for and standardize the generation of Financial Advisors' presentations to clients.
• Lead the design and development of the abovementioned Presentation Builder application.

1998–2000 Services Group

EDS – Senior Project Manager, Consumer Network Financial

• Managed the development of Web-based report rendering and repository applications.
• Implemented Web-based report repository in client banks and financial institutions.
• Conducted formal training for internal and external users in both English and Spanish.
• Matrix-managed six programmers.

1988–1998

Prudential Insurance Company of America
Prudential Preferred Financial Services – Project Leader/Senior Business Analyst, 1994–1998
Managed the implementation of a vendor-based, online testing application used by more than 4,000 advisors in 150 offices

nationwide: won the 1996 ASTD Blue Ribbon award in the Technology Based Performance Support category.

- Led team of programmers charged with developing Windows based applications providing financial and business management solutions to the company's Financial Advisors.
- Gathered business requirements; performed system analysis, design and prototyping; generated technical specifications; provided project planning and management functions; managed quality assurance testing; performed application implementation; authored user documentation; provided user training.
- Served as key member of corporate re-engineering team responsible for optimizing work process flows, creating job aids and training programs for field management personnel.
- Chosen by peers as Team Editor to assure accuracy and readability of team-generated documentation.

Prudential Capital Management Group - Business Analyst, 1990–1994
- Designed, developed, and implemented enhancements to Portfolio Management system handling over $12 billion in assets using RAMIS and SPX.
- Managed two programmers.

Prudential Group Operations - Programmer Analyst, 1988–1990
- Designed and developed applications to support an insurance administration and claims processing system using COBOL, CICS, and VSAM in MVS environment.
- Managed one programmer.

TECHNICAL SKILLS
Platforms   WINDOWS, UNIX
Software   MS-Project, MS-Access, MS-Excel, MS-Word, SQL, Unix scripting.

EDUCATION
1993–1995   <u>Rutgers University, New Jersey</u>
                 Thirty credits toward Master's Degree in Business Administration.
1983–1987   <u>Arcadia University, Pennsylvania</u>
                 Bachelor of Science Degree in Computer Science.
                 Minors in Business Administration and Mathematics.

> ADDITIONAL SKILLS THAT SUPPORT A CAREER IN MANAGEMENT.

Solid verbal and written communication skills.
Excellent interpersonal and analytical skills.
Fluent in Spanish, knowledge of French.

> NOTE THAT THIS RESUME VARIES ONLY SLIGHTLY FROM THE PREVIOUS VERSION. FOCUS ON THE VERBS—THE DIFFERENCES ARE IN EMPHASIS, NOT IN THE DETAILS OF ACCOMPLISHMENTS.

Chronological

An administrator planning a new career in sales.

ELLEN McSELLWELL

310 El Camino Road
San Diego, California 92103

Residence: (619) 555-0000
Business: (619) 555-0001
sellme@blah.com

> PARTICULARLY IMPORTANT TO STATE OBJECTIVE WHEN CHANGING CAREERS.

OBJECTIVE HOSPITAL AND MEDICAL SALES REQUIRING EXTENSIVE EXPERIENCE WITH STATE-OF-THE-ART MEDICAL EQUIPMENT, OUTSTANDING COMMUNICATIONS SKILLS, AND STRONG MOTIVATION.

PROFESSIONAL ACCOMPLISHMENTS

> CLEVER AND COMPETITIVE.

• Successfully conducted training seminars for nearly 200 supervisory personnel in interpersonal skills.
• Developed reputation for simultaneously coordinating numerous involved projects. Written up in Hospital Administrator magazine, 2006.
• Retained by three directors. Appointed to current position over fourteen other qualified candidates.
• Achievement-motivated, conscientious, objectives-directed. Obtained highest performance rating for three years.
• Adept at problem resolution and public relations. Regularly represent hospital at major civic gatherings.
• Experienced in the development of management systems, including the administration of a $4.3 million budget.
• Active member of Medical Equipment Review Committee, 2005–2007.
• Received U.S. security clearance.
• Experienced in the development of management systems, including the administration of a $4.3 million budget.
• Active member of Medical Equipment Review Committee, 2005–2007.
• Received U.S. security clearance.

> KEY STATEMENT FOR ANYONE WANTING TO BREAK INTO SALES.

EMPLOYMENT HISTORY

2005 – Present: Administrative Assistant to the Director, San Diego Memorial Hospital
2000 – 2005: Administrator to the Chief of Medical Administration, San Diego
1998 – 2000: Sold LaBelle health and beauty products door-to-door in West Virginia

EDUCATION
B.A., Administrative Management, 1998
Marshall University; Huntington, West Virginia
Additional course work at University of San Diego in Group Dynamics, Management, and Psychology

> UTILIZING SKILLS AND ACCOMPLISHMENTS TO CONSTRUCT A NEW CAREER.

ADDITIONAL EDUCATION

Advance Management
AMA Supervisory Skills

Hospital Supervision
Kepner-Tregoe Problem Solving

PERSONAL Able and willing to relocate and/or travel extensively.

> SALES-ORIENTED.

Combined

Transforming "housewifery" into job-related skills.

Lotta Toffer
327 Carmichael Avenue
Topeka, Kansas 66601
(913) 555-0000
E-mail: lotalots@aol.com

Objective   A challenging position that will both utilize and strengthen the organizational and motivational skills acquired in over eleven years of diverse, demanding responsibilities.

> CREATIVE STATEMENT TRANSLATING WORK EXPERIENCE INTO JOB-RELATED SKILLS.

Experience   Served over 11 years as a suburban homemaker and mother of three children with success and skill in the following areas:

> ACTION VERBS, IMPACT STATEMENTS.

- **Budgeting**—Accountable for the control and disbursement of an annual budget of $72,000; including filing tax returns.
- **Prioritizing**—Established schedules, met milestones, and coordinated diverse resources and inventory tasks.
- **Training and Supervision**—Trained, instructed, and directed three junior associates, whose training and development was under my jurisdiction, in a wide variety of skills (from bicycle riding and managing a paper-route to writing term papers).
- **Recruitment, Interviewing, and Selection of Personnel**— Hired a wide variety of professionals, including electricians, physicians, roofers, and baby-sitters.
- **Purchasing**—Analyzed and initiated purchases of low-budget to high-ticket items, including two automobiles, 950 square yards of carpeting, a twenty-four-cubic-foot freezer, orthodontic and medical services, and six rooms of furniture.

> VALIDATES CLAIM TO MANAGEMENT SKILLS.

NOTE: All the above was accomplished successfully while completing a two-year Associate Degree at Topeka Junior College (Dean's List five out of six semesters).

> NECESSARY DUE TO LIMITED WORKPLACE EXPERIENCE.

Excellent references available upon request.

Functional

Leaving the military to launch a business career.

Abel Baker

127 Hampton Street
Rockville, MD 20850

abcharlie@cap.org
Residence: (301) 555-3784
Answering Service: (301) 555-4895

Qualifications and Objectives   POSITIVE, CONVINCING, AND CAREFULLY TARGETED.

Being promoted all the way from the rank of staff sergeant to captain is a clear indication of reliability, leadership, and character. A decade of successful logistics management has prepared me to manage the transportation/trucking division of a medium-sized organization in need of cost efficiency and innovation.

Work Experience

COST SAVINGS.

CLEARLY STATED
EFFICIENCY.

• Organized, managed, and budgeted for a 140-vehicle transportation center with an annual operating budget of over $4 million.
• Initiated, developed, and directed a computer scheduling system that resulted in a 27% improvement of deliveries and an annual cost savings in excess of $600,000.
• Implemented a revised bidding system on the purchase of new vehicles, resulting in quicker purchase decisions and increased opportunity for price reductions.
• Effectively implemented personnel policies that led to a 19% increased efficiency rating over a two-year period. Received two commendations from management.
• Improved measurement and communication of safety-related issues, resulting in nineteen months of accident-free work activity (an all-time division record).

CONCISE, BALANCED, COMPREHENSIVE STATEMENTS.

Work History
2003 – Present: Regional Director, Transportation and Logistics Command, U.S. Army, Washington, D.C.
1999 – 2003: Director, Transportation Section, Fort Campbell, Georgia
1994 – 1999: Division Manager, Motor Pool, Fort Campbell, Georgia
1992 – 1994: Supply Officer, 3rd Army, Stuttgart, Germany

PROMOTED
THROUGH
THE RANKS.

ALWAYS LIST SUCCESSFUL MILITARY ACHIEVEMENTS.

Military Rank
Captain, U.S. Army

Education
Diploma, Greensboro High School, Greensboro, North Carolina

Foreign Languages
German   EMPHASIZES ATTENTION-GETTING SKILLS AND EXPERIENCE.

Combined

A retired law-enforcement officer seeks to extend his career.

Yu Sing Yee
200 Bay Bridge Avenue
Brooklyn, NY 11000

e-mail: *SgtYu@law.gov*
phone: 718/900-1234
cell: 917/700-4321

SUMMARY Recently retired member of the New York City Police Department. Achieved rank of Sergeant over an exemplary career of more than twenty years. Extensive experience in law enforcement and community relations.

PROFESSIONAL ACCOMPLISHMENTS

June, 2002–Present   Insurance Investigator, New York Life Insurance
Investigate insurance claims thought to be suspicious; uncovered 47 cases of attempted fraud resulting in savings of over $1 million.

Sept, 1980–May, 2002 New York City Police Department
Served with distinction over a period of twenty-two years.

> CONSISTENT UPWARD MOVEMENT THROUGH THE RANKS.

May, 1997–May, 2002   Sergeant, *Supervisor, Anti-Crime Unit*
Patrolled assigned neighborhoods in plain clothes to assure public safety. Identified and monitored targeted illegal activities.

> TRANSFERABLE MANAGEMENT AND SUPERVISORY SKILLS.

- Supervised four Police Officers.
- Evaluated performance of team members.
- Maintained administrative reports.
- Conducted investigations.
- Collaborated with interstate agencies and Police Departments.

July, 1995–May, 1997   Sergeant, *Patrol Supervisor*
Promoted to Sergeant: worked alternatively as Patrol Supervisor and Desk Officer.
- Coordinated daily activities of Precinct.
- Trained new Police Department recruits.
- Supervised up to thirty Police Officers.
- Evaluated performance of squad members.
- Verified arrests, provided emergency services, decided varied courses of action.

September, 1985 – July, 1995   Detective, *Brooklyn Night Watch*
Conducted preliminary investigations on all serious incidents, including homicides, serious assaults, bias incidents, and other major crimes. Responsible for analyzing crime scenes, interviewing complainants and witnesses, filing reports, and providing notifications to specialized units.

February, 1985 – September, 1985   Detective, *Precinct Detective Unit*
Promoted to Detective rank in December, 1984.

September, 1980 – December, 1984   Police Officer

EDUCATION   BS, John Jay College of Criminal Justice (plus extended credits in Accounting).

> STRONG ACADEMIC BACKGROUND.

FOREIGN LANGUAGES   Cantonese.

Chronological

An ex-offender seeking a brighter future.

Rex Conn

12591 Euclid Avenue
East Cleveland, Ohio 44112

bustout@freedom.com
Business: (216) 555-1261

Career Objective: *To apply my extensive firsthand experience in career and crisis counseling of ex-offenders and probationers, which helped them strengthen their lives and make positive adjustments to society.*

Experience:

COUNSELING: Considerable experience as a result of over 300 one-on-one counseling sessions with ex-offenders in the areas of career assessment and drug and alcohol abuse.

PROGRAM DESIGN: Initiated, designed, and implemented a career/life-planning workshop that resulted in nearly 46 probationary attendees participating: 22 landed jobs within six months of program completion.

LEADERSHIP: Headed up the Prison Reform Board, a sixteen member state organization designed to improve prison conditions and treatment of inmates.

HUMAN RELATIONS: Developed reputation in working with diverse ethnic/neighborhood groups to encourage probationary individuals to accept and profit from counseling. Written up in *Cleveland Plain Dealer* as a popular neighborhood activist.

MANAGEMENT: Lead counselor in evening crisis intervention center program. Under my guidance over a period of fourteen months, the center handled over 4,000 phone calls and 1,900 walk-ins.

CITIZENSHIP: Secretary for Cleveland Concerned Citizens, a civic organization dedicated to helping ex-offenders establish productive lives in the community.

MEMBER OF NATIONAL ASSOCIATION OF CAREER COUNSELORS

Education:

Bachelor of Science Degree, to be obtained June 2008, Cleveland State University
Major in Guidance and Counseling

ADDITIONAL EDUCATION: Crisis intervention workshop, through Ohio Guidance and Counseling Association, 2003; seminar entitled "Alcohol and Substance Abuse," sponsored by Cleveland Chapter of National Association of Career Counselors, 2003.

References:

Outstanding references available on request.

Functional

A technical consultant who has already made the change to management.

Ira Reese
4806 Alabama Avenue
Washington, DC 20019
(292) 583-1234

Overview   More than 25 years of business applications experience in all phases of project life cycle, with the past 8 years focused in the SAP environment.

Software   SAP R/3, ABAP/4, Oracle, COBOL, CICS, IDMS, VSAM, MVS JCL, TSO/ISPF, MS Office Suite, Visio.

Professional   **Sharp Electronics Corporation**
Experience   *SAP Lead Developer*
                                                               SAP Developer
> ORIGINALLY BROUGHT IN AS A CONSULTANT, HE IS NOW   *Project Leader*
> MANAGING A SOFTWARE DEVELOPMENT TEAM.   *Consultant*

Manage and collaborate in the design and development of conversions, interfaces, reports, and enhancements in support of five SAP implementation projects, a system upgrade, and many special project initiatives. As development team lead, conduct monthly meetings with business unit representatives to review requests and set priorities, assign resources, manage workload, and provide continuous 24-hour support coverage.

> THIS FORMAT IS AN ALTERNATIVE TO THE BULLETED APPROACH.

Actively participated in design, development, and implementation of the Order Processing and Accounts Receivable Systems for a major electronics manufacturing company. Systems consist of online transactions using COBOL, CICS and IDMS, and batch programs. Application areas included order processing, allocation, distribution, commission, and cash application. Project tasks included conducting user interface, system design, and program development.

Goldman Sachs   **Consultant**
Team member in design, development, and implementation of a Bank Loan Collateral Allocation System for an investment firm. System consisted of online transactions using COBOL, CICS and IDMS, and batch programs. Applications included bank account and loan maintenance and collateral allocation. Project tasks included conducting user interface, system design, logical database design, and supervising development team.

Purolator Courier   **Consultant**
With team members, developed and implemented Order Entry and Control System for express delivery service. System used IDMS and ADS/O transactions for customer maintenance, order entry, regular service, rate quotes, and points served. Tasks included designing screens and preparing program specifications.

> ACCOMPLISHMENTS PRESENTED IN CHRONOLOGICAL ORDER WITHOUT DATES.

A technical consultant who has already made the change to management.

Brooks Fashion Store   **Consultant**

With team members, developed Expense Payable System for a national chain of retail stores. System consisted of online transactions using COBOL, CICS and IDMS, and batch programs. Application areas included vendor and lease maintenance, monthly lease expenses, and construction project expenses. Project tasks included designing screens and program development.

CE Lummus   **Consultant**

With team members, developed construction phase of Material Management System for an international engineering company. System consisted of online transactions using COBOL, CICS and IDMS, and batch programs. Application areas included receiving, inventory, allocation and issue of materials. Tasks included preparing time estimates, scheduling assignments, and supervising program development.

Container Transport International   **Programmer Analyst**

Involved in design, development, and implementation of the Equipment Tracking System for an international transportation company. This system consisted of online transactions using COBOL, CICS and IDMS, and batch programs. Application areas included conversion and maintenance of customer, geographic, and equipment data. Tasks included screen design, preparation of program specifications, and program development.

Education   **Brooklyn College**
                         B.A. in Economics (Cum Laude)
                         New York University - School of Continuing Education
                         COBOL Programming
                         SAP Training
                         ABAP/4 Development Workbench, Dictionary, List Processing, Transaction Processing, Data Interfaces, Enhancements and Modifications, Communication Interfaces, SAPScript Forms, Application Link Enabling, IDoc Interfaces, Processes in Sales and Distribution (Sales, Delivery and Billing).

> THIS, AND THE SOFTWARE LIST ON PAGE 1, SERVE AS KEYWORDS.

Chronological

Consulting Resumes

Consulting resumes are significantly different from the types presented earlier. If you work as an independent contractor, vendor, free agent, consultant—however they refer to workers who are not employees in your neck of the woods—you need a resume that announces the full range of your skills and experience to the attention of decision-makers.

What to Include

Most consulting agencies and potential clients want to see employment history in chronological detail:

- The kind of work you've done (applications, purpose/use) recently and over a period of years
- The tools (especially technical) and techniques you are able to use
- Quantifiable results (such as completed projects on/ahead of deadline and within budget) and value-added (improvements, innovations, cost savings, and so on)
- Levels of responsibility (for instance, team/project leader, assigned responsibility for, and so on)
- Adaptability and problem-solving skills
- References and names of clients
- Keywords, including any specific and relevant technical, unique, or desired skills not otherwise listed within the body of your resume—it's best to include them under a heading titled "Special Skills" or something similar (rather than "Keywords").

Length

Elsewhere in this book we strongly recommend that traditional resumes (those written to attract full-time positions) generally be limited to one or two pages. Consulting resumes are an exception to this principle in that they need to exhibit the different kinds of contracts you have successfully completed, emphasizing those with the closest relevance to your current search.

The length and specificity of your consulting resume depends upon the nature and range of your accomplishments and of course the kind of work you are seeking. If your background and interests are uniquely focused in a few technical specialties, such as Java/HTML programming or an exotic area of bio-engineering, you may not need to broaden the scope of your resume. However, most consultants must be ready to adapt their resumes according to market needs and available openings.

Value Added

Senior consultants are expected to show an understanding of the priorities and business applications they helped to develop or improve. Value added, such as improvements to the project plan and suggestions that were implemented by the client, are likely to raise your perceived value above that of people who blindly follow instructions.

Problem Solving

Examples of problem-solving skills are usually the right consulting stuff: State the problem and how you resolved it clearly and succinctly. Remember, your explanations will not impress if they cannot be understood by less technical readers.

A retired executive seeking part-time consulting work.

Isaac E. Elder

25 Cedar Lane
Raleigh, NC 27602

Home: (919) 555-0001
olddude@neolith.com

Objective SPECIFIC AND DESCRIPTIVE.
To apply my extensive management, problem-solving, marketing and interpersonal skills in a consulting capacity to selected sales and marketing organizations.

ACCOMPLISHMENTS SUPPORT OBJECTIVE.

Summary of Accomplishments

- Doubled sales in capacity as marketing director during a down economy (2001–2007). CONSISTENCY.

- Redesigned and regrouped over 100 sales/marketing brochures into 20 coordinated pamphlets that won Marketing Age magazine's "Award of Excellence."

- Managed one of nine national sales regions consistently number one for 21 quarters (1985–1988).

- Active member of National Machine Tool Builders Association. Headed technical update subcommittee (1996–2002).

- Named St. Louis Business Alliance "Public Speaker of the Year" (1998 and 2001). PEOPLE SKILLS.

- Started St. Louis Business Alliance mentoring program linking over 300 volunteer executives with high school and college students.

- Recognized as developer of effective sales representatives. "Salesman of the Year" came from my region 3 out of 4 years. RESPONSIBILITY.

- Prepared, managed, and monitored corporate marketing budget exceeding $3.2 million.

- Developed and assisted in leading over 200 sales representatives through a 3-week "Sales Excellence" training program.

Employment history	CROSBY MACHINE TOOL CORPORATION; Abilene, Texas Marketing Vice President (2000–2006) McDOUGLAS AND CARTY CORPORATION; St. Louis, Missouri Sales Manager (1977–2000) U. S. ARMY — Lieutenant (1973–1977)
Education	B.S. — BUSINESS ADMINISTRATION; University of Kansas; Topeka, Kansas

A LONG AND SUCCESSFUL CAREER SUMMARIZED IN A SINGLE PAGE.

Combined

Tamara S. Leonthal
8888 Starfork Dr., Austin, TX 78759

(512) 414-1234
e-mail: *sar@aol.com*

SUMMARY   A CLEARLY STATED SUMMARY BACKED BY EXTENSIVE EXPERIENCE.

IT management; integration of IT into general business applications; large project management; Web, client/server and distributed processing development; data base systems; standards and processes; cross-platform (mainframe/mini/PC) systems.

PROFESSIONAL ACCOMPLISHMENTS   FULL-TIME EMPLOYMENT.

2002–Present   Metropolitan Transit Authority   *Senior Project Manager*
Project Manager for region-wide project:

- Coordinate activity of four independent governmental agencies.
- Review contractor proposal, negotiated contract.
- Review technical and project plans.   ACTION VERBS DESCRIBE ACCOMPLISHMENTS.
- Manage acceptance-test team.
- Monitor contract progress and payments.

2001   Morgan Stanley   AN INTERLUDE AS A CONSULTANT.   *Consultant*
Established Project Management Office:

- Created classification of projects based on size, risk, and related factors.
- Defined development and management procedures based on that classification.
- Reviewed/managed projects to effect transition to and compliance with new standards.
- Mentored Project Managers.
- Designed database for major project with ERWin.

BACK TO FULL-TIME EMPLOYMENT.

1999–2000   USWeb/CKS Cornerstone   *Senior Project Manager*
Managed team (employees and contractors) to determine business needs, define requirements, specify architecture, design/develop large (~200 screen templates, multi-platform back-end interfaces) Web-based, SQL server e-business product for major financial client.

- Determined and documented business requirements.
- Created information and infrastructure architecture.
- Defined programming and documentation standards.
- Directed screen treatment, design, and navigation.
- Designed and programmed Web site.
- Led employee training and development.
- Headed selection, sizing of hardware, software, and communications network.

A high-tech professional who switches between consulting and employment.

1999   Morgan Stanley | ANOTHER CONSULTING PERIOD. | *Consultant*

Assessed IT organization structure and recommended changes (organization, practices, and tools) to aid transition from legacy, mainframe-based development to RAD (Rapid Application Development), Client/Server, and Web-based development. Coordinated SEI CMM study.

1997–1999   New York City Transit Authority   *Special Consultant to CIO (VP)*

Redesigned technology infrastructure and software architecture. Created small client/server application to demonstrate new paradigm. Introduced Visual Basic, HTML, ActiveX. Supported data warehouse and digital imaging exploratory committees.

| A FULL-TIME MANAGEMENT POSITION. |

1991–1997   Cubic Corporation - MetroCard   *Software Director (80+ Staff)*

Senior IS executive (reporting directly to President) with P&L responsibility for development and operation of fare collection system for New York subways and buses. This was a large, complex, 24x7 system incorporating the latest technology including magnetic tickets and smart cards, consisting of IBM mainframes (MVS, CICS, DB2 & COBOL) hosting an LU6.2 WAN of PCs and AIX systems, each acting as a server with its own LAN of client devices in a client/server environment. System was developed by multiple teams on both coasts. Project delivered on time and within budget.

- Identified business needs and convinced client of their value.
- Defined requirements to satisfy agreed to business objectives.
- Contracted negotiations with client to deliver product that satisfied needs.
- Contracted negotiations with multiple subcontractors to develop portions of product.
- Designed, programmed, tested, installation and operation of automated system.
- Outsourced subsystem development.
- Coordinated efforts of multiple suppliers.
- Re-engineered accounting.
- Led acquisition and sizing of hardware and communications.
- Managed project totaling over $13 million billing; exceeded profit target.

Selected by chairman as part of special management team to create a new subsidiary corporation.

1982–1991   Computer Software Innovations Group, Ltd. | ENTREPRENEURSHIP. |
            Identified market needs and defined products for client companies.

1990–1991   Developed testing course for organizations using object oriented techniques. Invited to speak at Object Expo '92.

1990–1991   IBM subcontractor: Reviewed management of 200+ staff project to streamline management structure and procedures.

A high-tech professional who switches between consulting and employment.

1986–1991   Subcontractor to P&YI (under contract to MCI): Developed and taught courses in technical management, project planning, testing and quality assurance. Established QA organization. Defined methodologies and standards.

1986–1988   Bell Communications Research: Designed and developed business model and relational architecture for corporate database to be implemented in DB2. Selected CASE tool for requirements project. Taught use of UNIX.

1982–1986   Bell Laboratories: Researched and implemented effective transfer of software inspections and other software engineering and QA techniques to over 40 development projects involving over 1,000 staff members. Developed and taught inspections and testing courses. Measured results: 30% reduction in development time, 80% in error rates.

1974–1982   IBM Corporation:

1980–1982   Instructor, Systems   FULL-TIME EMPLOYMENT WITH INCREASING RESPONSIBILITIES.
• Designed and taught management and software engineering courses to senior data processing management and staff.
• Performed research in software engineering, identified best practices.

1978–1980   Systems Engineering Manager, N.Y. Banking Office
• Managed two teams of systems engineers: one of financial experts, the other technical specialists.
• Planned branch office staffing and training.
• Recognized as one of top 10% of IBM's S.E. Managers.

1976–1978   Teleprocessing Specialist, New York Region
• Reviewed/approved communication proposals and network design for technical accuracy.
• Conducted courses in Communications Management, SNA.

1974–1976   Project Manager, Financial Office

1974–1977
• Designed and managed implementation (in major New York City financial institution) of first SNA network shipped by IBM.
• Project delivered on time; the network and methods I developed were adopted by IBM as models for similar projects.

A high-tech professional who switches between consulting and employment.

EDUCATION AND HONORS

Cornell University

University of Connecticut

MA, Mathematics

IBM Management School

BS, Mathematics Cum Laude

IBM Systems Research Institute

Member, Sigma Xi, National Science Honorary Society.

Member, M.A.A., Mathematical Association of America.

> SOLID ACADEMIC CREDENTIALS.

PUBLICATIONS

"What's the Object," Object Oriented Hotline, December, 1991.

"Improving the Performance of Software Development Organizations," Computer-World, 2/19/1990.

ADDITIONAL KEYWORDS: Java Script, VB, Intranet, Internet, Web, Network, Data Warehouse, DHTML, XML, CSS, GUI, MS Office, MS Project, VBA, Word, Excel, VSS, Data modeling.

> A FEW ADDITIONAL KEYWORDS TAMARA DIDN'T MANAGE TO FIT INTO THE BODY OF THE RESUME.

Chronological

A technical management consultant who gets things done.

Shappa Lakota
5344 11th Ave S
Minneapolis, MN 55417
happytrails@tipi.com

SUMMARY A STRONG SUMMARY BACKED BY EXPERIENCE.

A highly motivated and seasoned professional with excellent communications skills, proven leadership abilities, and extensive experience in Information Technology.

ACCOMPLISHMENTS/CAREER HISTORY PROJECT AND RESOURCE MANAGEMENT.

4/2003–Present   **Senior Project Manager**

• Manage software development and installation projects for the Research Division of a large New Jersey–based pharmaceutical company: develop and track project plans and resources.
• Managed I/T Infrastructure components of projects, developed and implemented project plans and infrastructure resources.
• Managed Information Services Team: Mentored Project Leaders in the process and techniques of Project Management, managed testing of Intranet Portal application.

1/2000– 4/2003   **Program Director**

Implemented Program Management Office (PMO) for major insurance company for e-commerce, new technology conversion, and Internet development projects. Mentored project leads, developed project plans for 7 projects and reporting status.

11/1998–11/1999   **Project Manager**

Managed a Y2K (Year 2000) project for a division of a large New Jersey–based pharmaceutical company: implemented remediation of client-server applications and infrastructure, auditing of CRO for risk evaluation, overseeing validation protocol development, and development of contingency planning.

10/1997–10/1998   **Consulting Manager**

• Directed Southern Tier-New York office of a national consulting firm: supervised fifty consultants, maintained account responsibility for eight accounts.
• Managed Y2K (Year 2000) project for major New York Insurance company: supervised twenty consultants, mentored junior Project Managers, led Team Building effort and reorganization into software factory model.
• Managed a Phase I Y2K (Year 2000) inventory delivery engagement for Hospital organization. Recruited and mentored Project Manager for subsequent phases II/III.

6/1996–9/1997   **Principal Consultant**

Developed business applications solutions for Manufacturing company. Utilized MS/Access and interfaced with ORACLE databases in TCP/IP, Windows NT networked environment. Led projects for Corporate I/T including client/server, EDI, MS/Exchange and Windows NT rollout.

A technical management consultant who gets things done.

11/1994–6/1996   **Consultant**
Authored Strategic I/T plans for several local governments and manufacturing business units.
• Formulated full disaster recovery plan for a Town Government with mixed hardware platform.
• Implemented Novell Netware 4.x Local Area Network, integrating an AS/400 over an Ethernet backbone.
• Installed several Windows95 workstations, connecting into the LAN.
• Designed and administered multi-user relational database application incorporating automatic backup procedures.

RESPONSIBILITIES AND RESULTS IN DIFFERENT ENVIRONMENTS.

1990–1994   **Director of Information Services – Government Entity**
Directed I/T organization, including a data center and a staff of twenty in a successful, 24/7 operation.
• Led several high-profile projects including Image processing, Computer-Aided Dispatch, Geographic Information Systems, Financial/Human Resource System including re-engineering, multiple platforms, and client/server technology.
• Planned and updated data center, including new raised floor, HVAC, UPS, early fire detection, security, implementing new computing platform, and accompanying operating systems and high-speed data communications network.
• Developed full disaster recovery plan, including use of hot-site facility running multiple drills.
• Enhanced I/T revenue process to totally support $2M operating budget, while employing TQM principles, including service level agreements and customer satisfaction surveys.
• Served as President of the NYS Information Technology Directors Association, assisting in conference planning, NYS legislation lobbying, Vision/2000 projects and seminars.

PROFESSIONAL SEMINARS
Project Management
Quality Training for Managers
Managerial Leadership   ONGOING EDUCATION AND INTEREST.
Year 2000 Compliance
PMI: PM for the Experienced Professional
Applied 21 CFR Part 11 training
Multiple technical courses in Operating systems and networking

EDUCATION
Bachelor of Science, Management Information Systems: Carlson School of Management, University of Minnesota, Minneapolis, MN
Associate Applied Science in Network Engineering - Dunwoody College of Technology, Minneapolis, MN

Chronological

A seamless transition from full-time employment.

John M. Davis

247 Lawndale Avenue
King of Prussia, PA 19406

Phone: 610-247-3889
jmdenterprises@comcast.net

Senior Business Analyst

THIS CONSULTANT LETS HIS EXPERIENCE SPEAK FOR ITSELF.

For UBS Wealth Management   Weehawken, NJ   2006–2007

Authored Business Requirements Document for major Client Performance Reporting initiative. Delivered detailed business requirements to development group for all client exhibits, including:

- Delivered detailed business requirements to development group for all client exhibits, including specification of data sources, data values, interface requirements, and client statement mock-ups.
- Initiated and participated in meetings to provide clarifications, updates, additions, and changes.

Senior Business Analyst

LISTING YEARS WITHOUT MONTHS CAN COVER EMPLOYMENT GAPS.

For National City Bank   Cleveland, OH   2006

Documented Workflow Procedure for Split Year Reporting at National City Bank.

- Reviewed and recorded process requirements with project team and end users.
- Developed comprehensive Workflow document beginning with Environment Preparation and ending with Transition of Statements to Production.

Senior Business Analyst   Chicago, IL   2004–2005
For Lasalle Bank N.A.

Assumed major responsibilities related to installation of Maxim Partners Employee Benefit 5500 reporting application.

- Lead Data Mapping Team combining qualifying 5500 transaction data from legacy (OMNI) and current trust accounting systems (GlobalPlus™).
- Quality Assurance application testing (format, balance, and reconcile reports).
- Reconciled and Balanced production client 5500 report packages.

Senior Project Analyst
For Chase/JPMorgan   New York, NY   1999–2003

Member of Quality Assurance Team on installation project of Sungard GlobalPlus™ application:

CONSISTENT FORMAT OF SUMMARY STATEMENT SUPPORTED BY BULLETED ACTION.

- Quality Assurance Team Leader on Trade/Settlement Team.
- Quality Assurance Team Leader for Infrastructure Testing (batch process, various interface testing and analysis).

SPECIFIC RESPONSIBILITIES AND ACHIEVEMENTS.

A seamless transition from full-time employment.

- Team Leader for third level support of legacy Trust System (AMTrust™): prioritized and assigned issues to development team for resolution, reviewed corrective actions with technical team, communicated changes, and managed installation and validation process.
- Team Leader for Mutual Fund Project: coordinated assignments to Research Team, reviewed corrective actions identified by team, communicated changes to input groups, validated posting of changes.
- Ensured that Trust Systems Group within Enterprise System Solutions Division met all internal and external requirements for Y2K readiness.
- Contributed to Common Database Platform Project by consolidating Houston and New York databases.
- Analyzed and detailed methods for improving Production process relating to trading and corporate actions.
- Reviewed efficiency of overall operational flow for Trading/Settlement and Corporate Actions Areas.
- Analyzed decreasing reconciliation breaks and discrepancies in production process.
- Developed matrices for recommended flow to proactively avoid breaks.

Senior Project Manager
Fidelity Investments   Detroit, Michigan   1997–1998
Managed Comerica migration to Release 9, a Fidelity Investments™ (Advisor Technology Services, LLC) compliance solution for Year 2000 AMTRUST™ platforms. Coordinated all aspects of vendor representation, including:

- Y2K upgrade coding retrofits.
- Interface Y2K deficiency analysis.
- Test planning.
- Training for the implementation of the Y2K compliant software release.
- Managing efforts of three technical contractors and two business analysts on site.

Account Director - West Region
SEI Investments   Oaks, PA   1994–1997
Managed delivery of over 200 custom programs for 3 major acquisition projects (U.S. Bank, Wells Fargo and Union Bank of California). Efforts resulted in 5-year contract renewal.

- Resolved significant Union Bank of California client service issues and managed service expectations.
- Managed Wells Fargo Bank relationship from 1992–1997: Kept Wells Fargo strategically abreast of SEI's development plans while integrating Wells Fargo Bank's requirements.

A seamless transition from full-time employment.

Senior Manager, Client Services
SEI Investments   Oaks, PA   1991–1994
Stabilized relationship at U.S. Bank and First Interstate Bank (California, Oregon
and Arizona). Managed service team of 6 responsible for day-to-day service needs of
large West Coast clients.

Installations Manager
PREMIER SYSTEMS   Wayne, PA   1987–1991

Discovered, researched, and resolved over 200 outstanding post conversion tasks at
Premier Bank.
Co-authored Installations Guide for Premier System Trust Plus™ products.

Senior Technical Manager, Trust Systems
BANK OF AMERICA   San Francisco, CA   1984–1987
Managed multiple aspects of conversion project, including data capture, custom pro-
gramming and user training.
Awarded Quarterly Achievement Award for managing expectations between
Employee Benefit Trust Division and Trust Systems Group.

> IF POTENTIAL CLIENTS WANT
> ADDITIONAL DETAILS, THEY CAN ASK
> DURING THE INTERVIEW.

Chronological

Displaying years of experience and achievement.

Arthur D. Rosenberg

375 Grant Avenue, Cresskill, N.J. 07626   phone: 201-123-4567   *art.rosenberg@att.net*

PROJECT LEADER / ANALYST / TRAINER / DOCUMENTATION SPECIALIST
Project Management/Business Analysis
Testing/Training for End Users
User/Instructional Manuals

> THESE TOPICS CAN BE REARRANGED AS NEEDED.

SERVICE   Team and project management; business analysis and testing; assessment and creation of innovative documentation and training materials, compliance and requirements documents, RFPs, and proposals. Applications include a wide range of financial services, pharmaceuticals, telecommunications, insurance, sales and marketing, publishing, and human resources.

> A CLEAR SUMMARY OF SERVICES.

SOFTWARE   Most major Windows/DOS word processors, spreadsheets, and flow-chart tools.

PROFESSIONAL ACCOMPLISHMENTS

> THIS REPETITIVE FORMAT IS PREFERRED BY MOST CONSULTING FIRMS AND AGENCIES.

- For Union Bank of Switzerland: 9/06 – Present

Project leader for significant portion of $35 million IS Toolset development project. Responsibilities include scheduling, tracking deliverables, identifying and resolving issues.
- For Systems Unlimited: 9/05 – 9/06

Created operations and user manuals for internal use, and promotional user instructions for clients of computer security system vendor.
- For Time Inc.: 5/05 – 9/05

Developed/edited phased tasks, roles matrices, standards, and templates for group responsible for creating Web sites for *Time Inc.* magazines.
- For Credit Suisse-First Boston: 12/04 – 4/05

Revised/updated system functionality manual; reorganized and completely recreated operations guide for IT group supporting derivatives trading desk. Tasks required analysis of existing records, familiarity with links and flows, and interviewing support staff.
- For Viacom: 9/04 – 11/04

Coordinated Sarbanes-Oxley compliance project: collected, critiqued and provided feedback and remediation recommendations across IT divisions.
- For Schwab Capital Markets: 8/04

Performed scoping analysis of production support requirements for Technology Service Center providing support for Help Desk, Trading, Retail, and Institutional Support staff, and Connectivity and Disaster Support groups.
- For Pfizer: 3/04 – 7/04

Short-term project: Collaborated with HP consulting team to update project progress spreadsheets and diagrams for Steering Committee and team management reports.

Displaying years of experience and achievement.

- For Prudential Financial: 11/03 – 2/04

Updated and established business requirements standards in Mutual Funds Technology group for requirements intended to integrate acquisition of American Skandia funds. Applications related to mutual and pension funds trading, management, and maintenance.

- For Washington (DC) Metropolitan Transit Authority: 1/03 – 6/03

Created standards and guidelines to support different Project Classes based on the anticipated effort, criticality, difficulty, and other pertinent project characteristics. Intent was to avoid imposing burdensome standards on short, simple projects while ensuring that the more complex projects followed an appropriately rigorous development process.

- For Schering-Plough: 3/02 – 11/02

Created components of Project Life Cycle validation documents (Part 11 compliance) and related materials for a leading pharmaceuticals company. Designed and conducted software test scenarios. Reviewed source documents in Documentum, interviewed user groups, coordinated with technical and other team members. Analyzed and wrote Service Level Agreement (SLA) and Business Continuity Plan.

- For Prudential Securities: 3/01 – 2/02

Coordinated with business and programming departments on successful conversion of old (insurance division) client services package to correspond to securities-based system. Wrote detailed business requirements and specifications, participated in sign-off testing. Components included fees, statements, related internal and external online systems, money funds and sweeps, service and operations (voice response unit, trade desk, service center), notification to internal departments and external vendors.

- For Paine Webber (Business Systems Division): 4/00 – 2/01

Managed two interrelated projects for Wealth Management Group:

1. Collaborated with other department to create automated Presentation Builder for over 10,000 brokers. Wrote business requirements, negotiated modifications for in-house deliverable, then wrote requirements for Phase 2.
2. Researched products and services, performed proof-of-concept, and wrote business requirements for off-site development of Collaborative Workspace for High New Worth group. Scheduled and conducted presentations by selected vendors, created comparative technology and time/cost grids, recommended vendor, and successfully organized selection and project initiation processes.

Also contributed to multilingual communications flow with UBS following acquisition.

- For Enterprise Technology Corporation: 10/99 – 4/00

Documented customized trading and portfolio management systems for high-profile clients of financial consulting and software-development corporation. Also wrote promotional project descriptions and contributed to creation of new company Web site.

- For AT&T: 8/99 – 10/99

Wrote business requirements for Oracle-based online filtering system used to enable massive customer account migration.

Displaying years of experience and achievement.

- For Scholastic Books: 4/99 – 8/99

Researched and wrote business requirements document, design specifications, and presentation materials for major Web-based ordering system; member of team gathering and prioritizing user requirements. Organized and created applications development documents for Cybase application and related design documents.

- For AT&T: 10/98 – 3/99

Created interactive training tutorial for online filtering system used to enable massive customer account migration.

NOTE THAT MULTIPLE RESUME PAGES ARE COMMONLY REQUESTED IN ORDER TO ASSESS A CONSULTANT'S QUALIFICATIONS AND EXPERIENCE.

- For Citicorp: 2/98 – 9/98

Documented several highly visible software systems; defined and upgraded documentation standards; wrote QA, testing, and GUI development standards.

- For AT&T: 11/95 – 1/99

Member of project development and requirements team for major financial system. Documented and trained online and Web-based financial, sales, customer evaluation systems, and Y2K requirements. Wrote GUI, QA, and testing standards. Delivered online Help and tutorials. Designed and conducted user training classes.

- For Teleport Communications Group (TCG): 4/94 – 10/95

Documented several highly visible software systems; defined and upgraded documentation standards; wrote QA, testing, and GUI development standards; introduced online help documentation; edited department status reports.

- For Cubic Automatic Revenue Collection Group: 7/93 – 3/94

Tested and documented results for new fare collection system.

- For Deutsche Bank: 6/93

Created prototype for documentation of international (multilingual) trading system.

- For MTV/Viacom: 1/93 – 5/93

Hired and managed team of 8 consultants in testing, documenting, and training customized JD Edwards/Synon A/R installation. Organized testing and training schedules throughout system implementation. Member of project management team.

- For United Parcel Service: 4/92 – 12/92

Analyzed and rewrote portion of customized methodology, based on Catalyst (CSC Partners) and Method/1 (Arthur Anderson).

CLIENT LIST

Managed multiple projects; analyzed and documented a wide variety of applications; conducted classes and training seminars in PC hardware and software, mainframe applications and methodology to clerical, managerial, and technical staff at:

Washington (DC) Metropolitan Transit Authority	AT&T
The Port Authority of New York and New Jersey	Pfizer
Cubic Automatic Revenue Collection Group	Citibank
Morgan Guaranty and Trust Company	Time Inc.
Teleport Communications Group (TCG)	Scholastic
American International Group (AIG)	Viacom / MTV
Enterprise Technology Corporation	Paine Webber
University of Stockholm (Sweden)	Deutsche Bank

Displaying years of experience and achievement.

New York City Housing Authority
Lucent Technologies / Bell Labs
New York City Transit Authority
Marine Computer Enterprises
United Parcel Service (UPS)
U.S. Department of Education
Paladyne Software Systems
McGraw-Hill Book Company
Union Bank of Switzerland
Credit Suisse-First Boston
Comerica - Detroit Bank
Schwab Capital Markets

Purolator Courier
Delmar Publishers
Union College (NJ)
John Wiley & Sons
Systems Unlimited
Marsh & McLennan
Paramount Pictures
Information Science
Prudential Financial
Prudential Securities
Berlitz School (Paris)
Janssen Ortho-McNeil

A CREATIVE WAY TO LIST FORTY CLIENTS.

RELATED ACHIEVEMENTS
- Directed marketing activities for two international publishers of technical and educational materials.
- Supervised multinational staff at United Nations agency in Geneva, Switzerland.
- Published and marketed college textbooks and related educational materials.
- Translator/interpreter for Organizing Committee of Grenoble Winter Olympic Games.

EDUCATION
MA, English, French - University of Grenoble, France
BA, Psychology - University of California at Los Angeles

PROFESSIONAL ASSOCIATIONS
ICCA - Independent Computer Consultants Association
The Authors Guild, The Authors League

FOREIGN LANGUAGES
French, Spanish, German, Italian, Dutch, Swedish

PROFESSIONAL CREDENTIALS.

COMMUNITY SERVICE
Provide career-related seminars and training classes to a number of minority and professional groups and organizations.

PUBLICATIONS
BOOKS

LISTS OF PUBLICATIONS (PATENTS, ETC.) ARE CONSIDERED APPROPRIATE.

THE RESUME HANDBOOK
2008 (Fifth edition), Adams Media, Avon, MA
THE REQUIREMENTS OF PROGRAMMING, the first section (four chapters) of the book, ACE THE TECHNICAL JOB.
2000, McGraw-Hill Book Co., New York

Displaying years of experience and achievement.

PREPARING FOR A SUCCESSFUL INTERVIEW, initial chapter in the book, ACE THE TECHNICAL INTERVIEW.
2000 (4th edition), McGraw-Hill Book Co., New York
CAREER BUSTERS - 22 WAYS PEOPLE MESS UP THEIR CAREERS AND HOW TO AVOID THEM
1997, McGraw-Hill Book Co.
MANIPULATIVE MEMOS - **Control Your Career through the Medium of the Memo**
1994, Tenspeed Press, Berkeley, CA.
CHESS FOR CHILDREN AND THE YOUNG AT HEART
1977, Atheneum, New York

ARTICLES

CONTROL YOUR CAREER WITH MEMOS
National Business Employment Weekly (Published by the Wall Street Journal), May, 1995.
KEEPING YOUR JOB IN A TECHNICAL ENVIRONMENT
National Business Employment Weekly, February, 1987.
HOW TO BECOME A COMPUTER CONSULTANT
National Business Employment Weekly, September, 1986.
MAKING THE TRANSITION TO A TECHNICAL CAREER
National Business Employment Weekly, June, 1985.
RESUME STRATEGY
National Business Employment Weekly (3-article series), June, 1985.
HABIT UN-FORMING *(interviewing techniques)*
National Business Employment Weekly, March, 1982.

Chronological

CHAPTER FIVE
The Worst Resumes We've Ever Seen

If a good resume is a work of art, a bad resume is an envoy of self-destruction.

Why, year after year, do so many people continue to send out semiliterate and dysfunctional resumes when there is so much related information available in bookstores and on the Web? Possibly because they are too lazy to read, research, and seek advice; clearly they underestimate the importance of an attractive and effective resume.

Put yourself behind the reader's desk as you peruse the following examples. Would you devote even a small portion of your workday to interviewing these men and women?

These are five of the worst resumes we've ever seen, selected from thousands of misguided attempts at attracting the interest of potential employers. That they fail is obvious.

We'll discuss their flaws and show you how three of them could be successfully rewritten.

RESUME	Vinny Vaguely
PERSONAL:	Birth Date: February 25, 1979. Single. Good health. Willing to travel/relocate.
EDUCATION:	B.S. in Business Administration, Central Michigan University, with a major in finance, 24 credit hours; additional concentration in marketing and economics. Overall GPA 3.1. Date of graduation, May 7, 2001.
EXTRA-CURRICULAR ACTIVITIES:	Marketing Association, 2000, 2001 Finance Club, 2000–2001 Student Advisory Council, 2000–2001 Theta Chi Fraternity–Secretary, 2000 Rush Chairman, 2001
HOBBIES and INTERESTS:	Golf, bowling, softball, basketball, reading, and music
WORK EXPERIENCE:	2002–Warehouseman for Leaseway of Westland, MI 2003–Warehouseman for Leaseway of Westland, MI 2004–Warehouseman for Leaseway of Westland, MI 2005–Temporary Welding Inspector–Ford Motor Company (after being laid off, painted exteriors of homes)
ADDRESS:	Home: 66666 Fox Glen Farmington Hills, MI 48018 Phone: 313-666-0606, 313-666-0607
COMMENTS:	I feel that I am a dependable, personable, and hard working individual who could be an asset to your business.

Name: Vinny Vaguely

Vinny Vaguely's vitae could (and maybe should) have been written on a three-by-five index card, the ideal size for recipes and other nonessentials. Although Vaguely seems to feel that he'd be an asset to our business, he offers precious little data to support this optimistic view.

Now let's take an analytical look at what Vinny *did* include:

- Name: A resume is not the place for nicknames.
- Resume: We can guess what this was intended to be, so the label is superfluous.
- Personal: This information is unnecessary and inappropriate. Any such details that are included in a resume, for whatever reason, belong at the very end.
- Education: Solid credentials, but poorly presented.
- Extracurricular Activities: Okay, but "Related Activities" might appear more grown-up.
- Interests, Hobbies: Who cares?
- Work Experience: Last job should be listed first, and the same job need not be listed more than once. No mention is made of job responsibilities or accomplishments.
- Address: We finally discover where Vinny Vaguely lives. Of course, the address belongs up at the top.
- Comments: Unsubstantiated and unconvincing: we have no idea of what Mr. Vaguely has done or is capable of doing in the workplace.

Charles "Chucky" Confuser

Charles "Chucky" Confuser   Telex: Smartashell
Easy Street
Big Town, NJ 07990

Statement of Position
As of July 20, 2001
"U" are current unit valuations of relative worth to investor.

ASSETS
CURRENT ASSETS
Abilities Derived Through Current Major Classes
Technical Capabilities   U   55
Spirit of competition
 (less allowance for cooperation)   90
Communicative capacity   90
Background in business courses   **100**
Units from current major classes   335
Leadership/Decision Making Ability   **125**
 TOTAL CURRENT ASSETS   460
Health and Physical Attributes   100
Former Education   75
Determination, Self-Confidence, and Self-Support
 (net of realization of dependence on others)   125
Goodwill and Intangibles   **100**
TOTAL ASSETS   U   860

LIABILITIES AND STOCKHOLDERS EQUITY
CURRENT LIABILITIES
Amount Due Others for Maintenance of Interest and Self-Development U   235
Amount Due Work Experience   **115**
 TOTAL CURRENT LIABILITIES   350
Long-Term Debt to Supporters of Current Position   140
Debt Related to Mark 12:17   **110**
TOTAL LIABILITIES   600
STOCKHOLDERS EQUITY
Common Stock   55
Retained Earnings (to facilitate future development)   **210**
TOTAL LIABILITIES AND STOCKHOLDERS EQUITY   U   860

Name: Charles "Chuck" Confuser

Believe it or not, resumes like this really do turn up from time to time!

Our Chucky has obviously confused imagination and cleverness with the purpose of a resume, and a potential employer is unlikely to spend the time trying to decipher it. This is not to say that innovation and creativity are forbidden from resumes; however, they must be applied judiciously and intelligently to complement, not dominate, important and clearly organized information.

This document not only is *not* a resume, it doesn't come close to fulfilling the purpose of a resume. Even if someone took the trouble to try and figure out the "formula" (bear in mind the other stack of resumes waiting on the interviewer's desk), it provides no meaningful basis on which to evaluate the candidate's experience or abilities.

The lesson here is that a resume should offer its readers relevant information rather than test their patience.

If all of this were not enough, the use of a nickname is another no-no.

Eleanora Unsura
1404 Moore Ave.
Lincoln, MO 65438
(417) 555-1174
Social Sec. No. 390-92-0000

Level of Education: High School Harper Woods High School 4 years
Business School Hallmark Business Machines Institute 9 months
Course of study Computer Programming
Specialization Cobol & RPGII Languages
Career Objective To Work Hard and become a good Programmer
Possible Salary $15,000 to $20,000 a year
Employment Experience:
Present Employer Whall Security Corp.
Job Title Security Officer.
Date of Employment 12/27/2005. Current Salary of $4.25 an hour
Job Responsibility To Take care of clients property from Fire of Theft
Previous Employer Little Caecars Inc.
Job Title Store manager & pizza maker
Dates of Employment March, 1992 to November, 1994 Salary $180 a week.
Job Responsibility To make pizzas when busy and to do daily paper work.
Personal References: Billy and Jane Smith, 1403 Moore Ave. (across the street).

Truly Yours

Eleanora Unsura

Name: Eleanora Unsura

What's wrong with this little eyesore? Almost everything!

The major flaws are that it is grammatically awful: poorly punctuated, full of misspellings, and irritating to the eye. It goes on to flout, destroy, or ignore virtually all of the fundamental rules of writing a successful resume.

To mention just a few specifics:

- Salary (past, present and requested) should never appear upon a resume.
- If you insist on listing references on a resume (where they do not belong in any case), at least spell the name of your employer correctly.
- Everything is jammed together, making the resume difficult to read.
- Relevancies and irrelevancies are intermingled, and it is completely lacking in structure.

Ms. Unsura gives us no idea of what she may have to offer a potential employer. She would be well advised to solicit help in organizing and writing a resume with purpose and technique.

On the following page, we offer an alternative.

Eleanora Unsura

1404 Moore Avenue   (417) 555-1174
Lincoln, Missouri 65438

OBJECTIVE: A programming position allowing for professional skill devel
                    opment, multiple applications, and potential for career growth.

EMPLOYMENT   Whall Security Corporation–Security Officer
HISTORY:
2005–Present   • Provide security service to a variety of business clients,
                    including hospitals and manufacturers.
                    • Discovered electrical fire in early stages while on patrol at
                    Parkcrest Hospital, resulting in quick and easy smothering of
                    fire and saving potential loss of costly research equipment.
                    • Maintained perfect attendance record while employed at
                    Whall, despite working at least thirty hours/week and com-
                    pleting coursework at Hallmark.
                    • "Employee of the Month"—Recipient three times.

2003–2005   Little Caesar's Incorporated—Store Manager
                    Managed $515,000 annual receipt in a seven-employee car-
ryout restaurant.

                    • Reduced losses from incorrectly filled orders by redesigning
                    order form. This resulted in a 55% drop in losses.
                    • Appointed manager at age seventeen and while still a senior
                    in high school.

EDUCATION: Hallmark Business Machines Institute—2003.
                    Completed nine-month computer programming program with
                    a proficiency score on final testing of 92%.

                    Harper Woods H.S., 1999.
                    Graduated within College Preparatory Curriculum.

ACTIVE
INTERESTS: Computers, Internet.

Amazingly, this is the same Eleanora who authored the previous interviewer's nightmare. With some careful thought about her achievements, a touch of respect for the English language, some carefully chosen action verbs, and a logical format, Eleanora's resume has been transformed into a readable resume.

RESUME

I.M. Brusk   Department of Geography
123 S. Adams   California State University
Correl, California 91106   80 State College Avenue
(213) 000-0000   Fullerton, California 91106

EDUCATION

2000–2002	Economic Geography U.C. Berkeley Ph.D.
1997–1999	School of Business Administration & Economics California State University–Fullerton M.B.A.
1993–1996	Geography, Major–Economics, Minor B.A. University of Bristol (England) Special Honors

WORK EXPERIENCE

2004–present	Associate Professor Department of Geography California State University–Fullerton
2000–2004	Assistant Professor Department of Geography California State University–Fullerton
1999–2003	Instructor Department of Economics University of San Francisco

CONSULTING

2006–Present	Urban Econometrics Co., Fullerton, Ca.
2005–Present	Market Profiles, Inc., Tustin, Ca.
2005	Orange County Forecast and Analysis Center

AWARDS, HONORS

1997–1998	James P. Sutton Fellowship, U.C. Berkeley
1996–1997	Thomas and Elizabeth Williams Scholarship, Glamorgan City Council
1993–1996	Special Honors, University of Bristol

Name: I.M. Brusk

What a pity to portray an impressive record of academic excellence in such an unimpressive fashion.

This resume tells us that I.M. Brusk has earned an MBA, a Ph.D. and special honors. We can further decipher, with careful study, that I.M. was promoted from assistant to associate professor.

The rest is speculation. Has this academic published? What courses and seminars has he/she taught? What are his/her academic and scientific specialties? What was the nature of his/her consulting? Has he/she any noteworthy research in progress? What, if any, are his/her goals? Why, we don't even know his/her first name.

Presumably, Professor Brusk is looking for a highly specialized position. However, there are other qualified people out there with Ph.D.s and honors of their own in competition. Given similar academic credentials, those whose resumes present them in a brighter light are likelier to win the interview.

Our advice to I.M. Brusk is to rewrite this resume with the elements we've outlined in *The Resume Handbook*. It might look something like the one on the following page.

ISABELLA M. BRUSK

123 South Adams
Correl, California 91106

Residence: (213) 000-0000
Work: (213) 000-0001

EXPERIENCE

2000–Current   California State University–Fullerton, Associate Professor, Department of Geography. In charge of curriculum development for department covering over 3,700 students annually. Personally direct nine yearly department classes, including newly designed class entitled "Changing Weather Patterns–Dawn of a New Age."

- Co-authored "Economic Cycle Influences of Changing Political Boundaries," a highly acclaimed series of articles appearing in July–October 2006 issues of the *Research Economist.*

Selected as:

- Member of Governor's Council on Earthquake Readiness, a sixteen-member task force of business, academic, and government people assessing current state readiness regarding safety, economic disruption, and proposed construction considerations. Youngest member of panel.
- Rated 96.4 out of 100 by nearly 750 students attending my classes during 2003–2006 (a rating of 90 is considered "outstanding.")
- Developed and tested computer model identifying economic trends (such as unemployment rates, median incomes, others) caused by changing populations. This was accomplished during a consulting assignment with Urban Econometrics, Fullerton, CA.
- Conceived, designed, and sold predictive voting model that pinpoints political voting trends utilizing demographics rather than polling. This predictive model has accurately predicted twenty-seven out of twenty-nine county races from 1995–2005.

1990–2000   University of San Francisco, Instructor–Department of Economics. Responsible for leading one senior-level undergrad and two graduate-level Microeconomics classes involving 120+ students.

- Developed instructional curriculum for sixty-hour class entitled "Economic Patterns and Their Historical Perspectives."

Member, American Association of Geographers

page 2

LANGUAGES: Welsh, French

PUBLICATIONS
1. *Hydrological Implications of Geothermal Developments in the Imperial Valley of Southern California*
   with G. George, R.H. Foster, and D.K. Todd
   Sea Water Conversion Laboratory, UCB, Richmond, November, 2000.

2. *1997 Population Estimate* with G. George and G. Britton
   Report on the Status of Orange County, 2002. Working Document No. 1, Forecast and Analysis Center, Orange County, CA.

3. *The Frequency of Social Contracts within a Time-Space Framework*
   with G. George
   Submitted for publication.

PROFESSIONAL PAPERS

1. *Intra-Urban Interaction and Time-Space Budgets* with G. George, D. Shimarua, and P. Barry
   Association of American Geographers, New Orleans, 2006.

2. *The Soviet Concept of Optimal City Size* with G. George and C. Zumbrunnen
   Association of American Geographers, New Orleans, 2004.

EDUCATION

Ph.D.—University of California at Berkeley, 2002: Economic Geography

M.B.A.—California State University–Fullerton, 1999

B.A.—University of Bristol (England), 1996: Geography Major, Economics Minor. Graduated with honors.

We discover not only that Professor Brusk is named Isabella, but we also gain a wealth of important information omitted from her initial resume.

We learn about her areas of expertise, that she has published extensively, and that she appears to be quite popular with her students.

Dr. Isabella Brusk, we find, has been appointed to a government panel; she is familiar with state-of-the-art techniques (computer modeling), and she has held consulting positions with private firms (no "bookish academic," our Dr. Brusk). Notice how her limp and lifeless resume has morphed into one that will demand its share of recognition in a fiercely competitive market.

Bart Bonehead

RESUME
OF
BART BONEHEAD

RESIDENCE:
808 Hopkins Drive East
Windsor, Ontario

OFFICE:
Graduate School of Business Administration

University of Windsor
Windsor, Ontario

PROFESSIONAL EXPERIENCE:

2004 to Present	University of Windsor, Windsor, Ontario
2004 to Present	Director of Placement, Graduate School of Business Administration, University of Windsor
2003 to 2004	Director, BBA Internship Program, Dearborn, Michigan Campus
2003	Substitute Teacher Windsor Public Schools Windsor, Ontario
2001 to 2003	Training Manager Hespin & Marquette Windsor, Ontario
1999 to 2001	Home Economics Teacher Weaton Public Schools Weaton, Ontario

EDUCATION:

University of Windsor, Windsor, Ontario; Master of Business Administration, 1998.
Major: Industrial Relations

University of Buffalo, Buffalo, New York; Bachelor of Science, 1996. Major: Secondary Education

EXCELLENT REFERENCES AVAILABLE UPON REQUEST

Name: Bart Bonehead

This resume is probably the most frequent, and thus typical, form of resume failure we've encountered. At first glance, it may not seem so bad. In fact, you may be saying, "Gee, that looks like my resume!"

Indeed, Bonehead's offering is not as obviously awful as some of the preceding examples of bad resumes. Its failure is more subtle and insidious, which is why we consider it more dangerous than the others. The problem isn't what you see, but rather what you don't.

At second glance, this sad excuse for a resume might be better suited to a footnote to Bart's career—it offers little more than the stuff of which memories are made. What, if anything, has he accomplished in his profession? Has he met with any noteworthy success? There must be *something* he has done over the years to interest a potential employer, but we can't find it here.

Other than where Bonehead has been, and when, this document provides job titles, identifies itself as his resume, and promises good references to anyone who might be interested. Fortunately, we know Bart well enough to help him out of his predicament, and so we took the time to rewrite his notes into a solid resume. They hardly appear to describe the same person.

Bartholomew X. Bonehead

Bartholomew X. Bonehead

808 Hopkins Drive East   Residence (519) 101-0001
Windsor, Ontario 74R 01S   Business (519) 010-1000

PROFESSIONAL OBJECTIVE

Attainment of a managerial level position as a Programs Director, Project Manager, or Section Head within a major university where my array of administrative, analytic, planning, and leadership skills can be fully utilized.

EDUCATION

M.B.A., University of Windsor, Windsor, Ontario—1988. Concentration in Industrial Relations. B.A., University of Buffalo, Buffalo, New York. Major in Industrial Relations.

B.S., University of Buffalo, Buffalo, NY—1996. Major in Secondary Education.

SIGNIFICANT EXPERIENCE

MANAGERIAL—Successfully headed twelve-member, $540,000 annual budget placement function; increased enrollments 1,147 over last four years at a 9,000-student university.

SYSTEMS DEVELOPMENT—Conceptualized and implemented computerized records system projected to save $175,000 in administrative expenses over next three years.

FUNDS DEVELOPMENT—During two-year assignment as BBA Internship Program Director: Established 359 successful corporate relationships totaling 577 students, resulting in additional bottom-line impact to university of $205,000.

PROGRAM DESIGN—Originated and initiated Student Enrollment Campaign involving promotional literature, student contacts at high schools and junior colleges, and direct mail: resulted in increase in enrollment during 2005 of 660 over 2004.

TRAINING DESIGN—Designed Comprehensive Management Program affecting 275 individuals covering all phases of management from planning to controlling for major Canadian retailer.

TEACHING EXCELLENCE

Runner-up (2003) as Teacher of the Year in a school district with 150 high school teachers.

POSITIONS

2004–Present	University of Windsor, Windsor, Ontario Director of Placement, Graduate School of Business Administration
2003–2004	University of Michigan, Dearborn Campus, Director of BBA Internship Program
2003	Substitute Teacher, Windsor Public Schools
2001–2003	Training Manager, Hespin & Marquette Ltd., Windsor, Ontario.
1999–2001	Home Economics Teacher, Weaton Public Schools, Weaton, Ontario

---

In contrast to Bart's original attempt, his rewritten resume shows that his work experience included significant managerial, fiscal, teaching, and operational responsibilities. In the first resume, his job progression appears sketchy and undefined. The improved version shows us a logical progression toward the position he is now seeking. Bart's new resume is an interview-getter.

Bottom Line

Even losing resumes can be transformed into winners!

All you need are a few uninterrupted hours of honest reflection, an understanding of how your background can appear to make you valuable to a potential employer, and a quick review of the basic resume guidelines outlined in Chapter 2. The rest is personal: choosing the format, typestyle, and layout that you feel best suits your background, and avoiding the pitfalls of poor resume writing.

Except for the brief final chapter on resume layout and design, this is our final word on successful resumes. The examples we have given you will hopefully provide the tools you need to create your own, unique profile.

However, we are not quite finished. In the following chapters, we'll talk about design and layout, and then focus on the two essential resume companions: the cover letter, and the personal sales (or broadcast) letter. After that, we will cover networking and a few other job-getting and changing activities.

CHAPTER SIX
Presentation

An ugly resume is less likely to be read than one that pleases the eye. This chapter will help you to structure your resume in a manner that is visually appealing and complementary to your background.

Typeface

The first thing to consider is your choice of typeface. You want your resume to stand out, not compete with movie or funeral announcements. Our advice is that you stick to a simple, clean typeface like Arial, Times Roman, or Helvetica. They are our choice because of their simplicity of design and clarity.

Another trap to avoid is combining different typeface styles (like Times Roman and Helvetica). Each of these typefaces offers a variety of light, italic, and bold that can be combined to produce an attractive visual effect.

Length

Debate continues as to whether resumes must be limited to a single page. Our point of view reverts to common sense:

- If your work experience is limited, that is, you are a recent graduate or have only held one or two jobs, there is probably no reason for your resume to exceed a single page. So if you can reasonably limit your resume to one page, do so.
- If you have held a number of positions and cannot properly describe your accomplishments and responsibilities on one page, then two pages are certainly acceptable. However, you do not need to provide detailed descriptions of jobs that date back more than eight or ten years, unless they add something significant to your experience and qualifications. Be sure to emphasize your most recent experience.
- Attachments, such as additional pages of publications (for writers, researchers and academics), may be appropriate.
- Exception: Consulting resumes are expected to include all relevant experience, even if they extend to multiple pages.

Layout

When you design your resume, bear in mind that open spaces make it easier to read. Avoid cramming your page(s) with heavy masses of print. For example, compare Eleanora Unsura's two resumes in Chapter 5.

Paper

Standard office stationery is the safe choice of paper on which to print your resume and cover letter, although a quality paper stock may improve the overall effect. Slightly off-white paper is acceptable, but beware of using pastels or darker colors, which look unprofessional.

Print as many originals of your resume as you need on attractive, letter-quality paper. Never send photocopies of your resume to a potential employer. They're okay for friends or employment agencies but not the person with whom you want to win an interview.

Bear in mind that your resume may be photocopied by a personnel department, and subsequently passed along to other members of their firm: Copies made from copies can lose readability. In an emergency, some professionally maintained office photocopiers may do a good job, but we think it's better to avoid potential problems by always having "perfect" copies of your resume on hand.

Accuracy

A final word: Proofread your resume at every step in the process, and ask a knowledgeable friend or colleague to help. Mistakes on resumes are embarrassing and unacceptable. No matter how much you pay to have your resume created, you're the one who loses if it isn't right. So be meticulous and don't settle for less than the very best. By way of example, look at the before-and-after versions of E. N. Trepreneurial's resume.

Before:

E. N. Trepreneurial

3000 High Expectations Way
Southfield, MI 48075
810-555-1122

CAREER SUMMARY

Twenty-three years of experience as an owner/executive of various types of companies including high technology, real estate services, and manufacturing.

EXPERIENCE

ENTREPRENEURIAL VENTURES, INC./COMMUNITY OF HOMES STUDIO,
President and Founder
Entrepreneurial Ventures is a consulting company specializing in sales generation and growth (including turnarounds) locally, nationally, and internationally. Company manages all phases of marketing and management of approved plans. Client companies are start-ups through large international corporations that are in need of immediate attention and/or growth.

Company also arranges Venture Capital, equity financing, debt financing, mortgage, lease, etc. financing through Venture Strategies, Inc., an investment banking firm in Southfield, Michigan. Entrepreneurial Ventures assists automotive, manufacturing, real estate/building, computer/software, high tech, health care, robotics, electronics, publishing, consumer products, and service companies.

Community Of Homes Studio was a company financed and managed by Entrepreneurial Ventures. Community Of Homes Studio had the largest indoor showroom of modular homes in the U.S. (93,000 sq. ft.). Featured ten homes that were landscaped and decorated in a village-like atmosphere with pond and waterfalls. Facility also had displays, mortgage companies, insurance companies, employment agencies, credit counselors, builders and developers, a restaurant, and day care. Activities involved housing financing as well as community affairs and parties. First six weeks generated 1,643 mortgage-approved buyers.

ENTREPRENEURIAL COMMUNITY HOMES, President and Founder
Manufactured housing company that erected homes in subdivisions and scattered lots in eleven counties near metro Detroit.

ENVIRA CORPORATION, President and CEO
Research and Development Company specializing in aerospace remote sensing and image processing. Responsibilities included commercializing scientific developments with oil and gas companies, Department of Defense, medical institutions and other governmental agencies.

ZANADU INTERNATIONAL, Executive Vice-President and Co-Founder

Washington company that provided electrical and electronic components to the lighting industry. Responsibilities included strategic/business planning and day-to-day general management with over 500 people in twenty-four offices in the United States and London, England. Growth from start-up to $78 million in sales in three-year period.

COMMUNITY CONSTRUCTION COMPANY, President and Founder

Home building company that constructed over four hundred residential homes, numerous condominiums, and several light industrial buildings in Metropolitan Seattle. Responsibility was overall management.

VILLAGE MANAGEMENT CORPORATION, President and Co-Founder

First condominium property management company in Washington.
Customers included Hanson Homes, Hobbs & Cintas, Lewis & Lewis, and Allison Development. Managed maintenance, insurance, banking, repairs, construction, and developer relations. Company managed over 6,000 units and expanded operations to include condominium sales.

BENNINGTON INTERNATIONAL INC., Vice President

Marketing and Sales Manager, Ohio Division. Managed three used home sales offices consisting of over one hundred sales and administrative personnel. Also, was responsible for Bennington - New Town, a 61,000-acre development of residential and commercial property in Lester Township, Illinois. Responsibilities included planning, land development, municipal relations, serving on homeowners association, antique village (thirty-acre amusement and historical village), marketing, and supervising commercial and residential sales. Also managed two other land developments in the Bloomington area.

Sales/Marketing Manager, Bennington - New Town. Responsible for all new home building activities as well as commercial land sales. Duties included contracts, pricing, floor plans, home closings, builder relations, warranty, broker relations, advertising and promotion, and sales staff management.

After:

Elias N. Trepreneurial
3000 High Expectations Way
Southfield, Michigan 48075
810-555-1122

CAREER SUMMARY

Twenty-three years of experience as an owner/executive of various types of companies including high technology, real estate/building, services, and manufacturing.

EXPERIENCE

ENTREPRENEURIAL VENTURES, INC.   **President and Founder**

Entrepreneurial Ventures *is a consulting company specializing in marketing and sales generation/growth through local, national, and international sales organizations. Client companies are startups through large international corporations that are in need of immediate attention and/or growth (including turnarounds). Entrepreneurial Ventures manages all phases of marketing and management of approved action plans. Entrepreneurial Ventures assists automotive, manufacturing, real estate/building, computer/software, high tech, health care, robotics, electronics, publishing, consumer products, and service companies.*

Entrepreneurial Ventures arranges Venture Capital, equity, debt, or mortgage/lease financing through Venture Strategies, Inc., an investment banking firm in Southfield, Michigan.

- Company provides Staff, Board of Directors, and/or Advisory Boards with national/international experience.

COMMUNITY OF HOMES STUDIO   **President and Founder**

Entrepreneurial Ventures financed and managed **Community of Homes Studio**, which had the largest indoor showroom of modular homes in the U.S. (93,000 square feet), featuring ten homes, complete with landscaping and interior design, in a village-like atmosphere with pond and waterfalls. Facility also had displays, mortgage/insurance companies, employment agencies, credit counselors, builders and developers, a restaurant, and a day-care center. Activities involved housing, financing, and community matters.

- First six weeks generated 1,643 mortgage-approved buyers
- First in country to include layoff insurance for purchasers guaranteeing payment of the homeowners' day-to-day expenses; for instance, health insurance, mortgage, utilities, and day-care providers
- Manufacturing capacity of sixty-two modular homes complete with site setups per week

ENVIRA CORPORATION   **President and CEO**

Research and Development Company specializing in aerospace, remote sensing, and image processing. Responsibilities included commercializing scientific projects with oil and gas companies, Department of Defense, medical institutions, and other governmental agencies. A subsidiary, a bio-tech company, was publicly traded.

- International leader in three-dimensional imaging of vision for the robotics and automotive industries.
- Leader in the monitoring of ice, icebergs, and their flows.

ZANADU INTERNATIONAL   **Executive Vice-President and Co-Founder**
Washington company that provided electrical and electronic components to the lighting industry. Developed strategic/business plans and managed over 500 people in twenty-four offices throughout the United States and London, England.

- Startup company that grew to sales of $78 million in three years.
- Sold products to over ninety foreign countries including England. 10 Downing Street was a customer.
- Rated as the fastest growing company in Washington.
- Research and development division develops products in conjunction with Motorola.

COMMUNITY CONSTRUCTION COMPANY   **President and Founder**
Home building company that constructed over 400 residential homes, numerous condominiums, and several light industrial buildings in Metro Seattle. Company owned three divisions; a real estate brokerage, a mortgage company, and an equity finance company.

- Largest speculative builder in the state of Washington.
- Grew from a single real estate office to become the largest lister/seller of residential properties in the state of Washington in first three months of operation.

VILLAGE MANAGEMENT CORPORATION   **President and Co-Founder**
First condominium property management company in Washington. Customers included Hanson Homes, Hobbs & Cintas, Lewis & Lewis, and Allison Development. Managed maintenance, insurance, banking, repairs, construction and developer relations. Company managed over 6,000 units and expanded operations to include condominium sales.

- Expansion of the landscaping/maintenance division allowed service to thousands of apartments and commercial accounts.
- Janitorial subsidiary serviced in excess of 700,000 square feet of offices.

BENNINGTON INTERNATIONAL INC.   **Vice President**
Consisted of a real estate sales office primarily for used homes in Bennington - New Town, a 61,000-acre development of residential and commercial property in Lester Township, Illinois, that included an antique village (thirty-acre amusement and historical village), builders, mortgage companies, marketing and commercial/residential sales, and a community development company that developed properties in Puerto Rico and Florida.
Marketing and Sales Manager, Ohio Division. Managed three sales offices consisting of over 100 sales and administrative personnel, New Town operations, and two other land projects in the Bloomington area. Duties included planning, land development, and maintaining municipal/ homeowners association relationships.
Sales/Marketing Manager, Bennington - New Town. Responsible for all new homebuilding activities as well as commercial land sales. Duties included contracts, pricing, floor plans, home closings, builder relations, warranty, broker relations, advertising/promotion, and sales staff management.

- Largest developer of year-round single family housing in Florida.
- Developer/builder of El Conqueror Resort in Puerto Rico.
- Owner of 40,000 acres in Michigan, Florida, South Carolina, North Carolina, Georgia, and Barbados.

CHAPTER SEVEN
Using the Internet

The Internet has revolutionized the way many people look for work, and also the way companies and agencies seek employees. Failure to recognize and make use of the greatest innovation since fermented grapes may leave you somewhat isolated.

The Internet is the fastest way to deliver your resume to potentially interested parties. Aside from speed, the pros and cons of using the Internet to circulate your resume and enhance your job search are fairly balanced.

The Pros

Tens of thousands of career-related Internet search engines, services, directories, and related sites proliferate on the Web. Online recruitment is by now a fact of life, and if your resume isn't out there, you may be missing out on valuable and viable opportunities.

Contrary to popular assumption, an online resume need not differ in content from the "traditional" version. Both should contain the keywords that characterize your experience and skills; both should allow recruiters and potential employers to quickly and conveniently evaluate your suitability for their needs; and both should follow the other rules and common-sense guidelines that define a good resume.

The Cons

Privacy restrictions vary among sites, and your control over where your resume is posted and who can see it may be limited. The shotgun approach leaves you vulnerable to unwanted headhunters and inappropriate job leads, not to mention your current employer. In addition, any updated versions that you post may coexist with earlier versions, creating inevitable confusion. You are advised to post your resume only on sites that guarantee tight privacy restrictions, although even these are questionable. Post updates periodically on a site that automatically deletes (or allows you to delete) previous versions, and find out if/how much they charge for updates. Remember to remove your resume from online sites when your job search is concluded.

Formatting restrictions may not allow for bold or underlined text, bullets, and other characteristics. Thus your online resume may not have the same look and feel as you might wish. Also, an online resume is not tailored toward a specific target, so you lose the ability to emphasize certain skills and interests over others.

Headhunters stalk the Internet, often late at night, looking for candidates with hot technical and other specialized skills. Posting your resume may get you bombarded with calls, some of which may be inappropriate or unwelcome.

Reality

It is comforting to believe that your resume is out there making the rounds of highly motivated recruiters and interested companies, but do not be lulled into a false sense of security. Online services are only additional resources, not a guaranteed pipeline to gainful employment. Continue to explore the old, traditional methods like networking, headhunters, and selected job listings.

Resources

We offer no recommendations, but some of the most popular Internet job-search resources include those offered by Truecareers.com, Careerjournal.com and Careerjournaleurope.com, Monster.com, Indeed.com, and Simplyhired.com. You can also find many resume-posting resources by searching on keywords like jobs, job boards, job search, resume banks, and various combinations of these and related words. Measure their claims with a healthy skepticism until they prove themselves reliable.

Online Research

The Internet is as close to a perfect research tool as you may find in an imperfect world. Searches that formerly took hours can be completed in minutes or seconds on the Web. If you do not have frequent occasion to use the Internet, practice by searching for different kinds of information, like making travel plans and doing historical or geographic searches. This will help when you need to find important information.

Recognize the Internet for what it is (a great resource) and what it is not (a replacement for personal contact).

Keywords

Today's employers tend to use keywords as a preliminary step toward identifying potential candidates. This is done both on the Web and within the databases of placement agencies, recruiters, and personnel departments.

Keywords are (usually) nouns that refer to specific tools and software products like Sun and IBM, Unix and Oracle, programming languages like C++ and SQL, certifications like Series 7, and applications like finance, portfolio management, telecommunications, biology, transportation, and so on. You need to know the keywords specific to your job-search arena in order to include the ones that belong on your resume.

There are two general techniques for including keywords: within the context of your job descriptions and in a separate paragraph under the heading, "Keywords." Obviously, using these words within a meaningful context will enhance both clarity and credibility.

E-Mail Cover Letters

The main difference between snail-mail and e-mail cover letters is brevity and format. Think of your e-mail cover letter as an abbreviation of the latter, and you will be on track.

From the perspective of the recruiter or hiring manager who receives the letter, the purpose of a cover letter is to help them to decide whether or not to take the time to view your resume. Most will not bother to open resumes received without a cover letter, much less those accompanied by a cover letter that fails to catch their interest.

The most convenient way to write a good cover letter is to compose and save a boilerplate version (or multiple versions). You can modify it to suit each occasion, with the advantage of a spell-checker.

Here are the rules:

- When e-mailing your resume to a specific individual, always cover it with a letter.
- Use the subject line to briefly introduce yourself and/or refer to any previous contact (such as a phone call).
- Elaborate with a sentence or two on the subject line, express interest (in the recruiter or company), refer to the attached resume, and sign off with enthusiasm.
- If appropriate, briefly explain why you are writing, who referred you (or where you got the person's name and e-mail address), and one or two skills or achievements that might attract their attention.

Example #1
A Personal Promo Cover E-mail

To: Arthur C. Reese

Southwest Tooling Research, Inc.

From: Ann Carmichael

> BOTH E-MAIL ADDRESSES AND THE DATE ARE AUTOMATICALLY POPULATED.

Mr. Reese,

> STICK TO FORMAL ADDRESS, EVEN THOUGH MANY PEOPLE DON'T. COURTESY IS NEVER INAPPROPRIATE.

Read with great interest your recent article in *Engineering Today* entitled, "Southwest Tooling's Push to Maintain Engineering Excellence."

I am frankly intrigued by your team research concept. The attached resume demonstrates my extensive, long-range commitment to tooling research and my own experience working with the team research concept.

> OKAY TO ABBREVIATE HERE, BUT NOT ON RESUME.

It is clear that you are looking for the best available people.

I feel that I can offer you a high degree of excellence.

Will follow-up early part of next week. Hope we can arrange an interview.

Ann Carmichael

Contact Information:
100 Valley View Terrace
home: (417) 555-4414
Santa Fe, NM 80801
AnnC@overview.com

> E-MAIL COVERS ARE NOT EXPECTED TO BE AS LENGTHY AS PAPER LETTERS. THE IDEA HERE IS TO INCLUDE RELEVANT FACTS AND ELIMINATE THE FLUFF.

Example #2
A Cover E-Mail to a Consulting Company

To: Mike Ramchip   From: Melvin Marvelous

Texas Techies

Mike,

I'm a senior Web developer with Java, HTML, XML, Active X, ASP, JSP, and CGI.

Have developed interactive sites for sports programs and professional team org. Resume attached.

Prefer consulting work, willing to consider full-time in Houston area.

-Mel

Contact:
100 Overland Trail
(866) 597-7777
Houston, TX 77090
Marvelocity@TTT.net

> E-MAIL TO A "HEADHUNTER" CAN BE EVEN MORE
> INFORMAL THAN IF ADDRESSED TO A PROSPECTIVE EM-
> PLOYER. IN FACT, MOST TEND TO APPRECIATE BREVITY.

CHAPTER EIGHT
The Art of Networking

Your resume has minimal impact on the success of your job search unless it finds its way to the right individual. Networking is one of the best ways to reach the people who can hire you, and many professionals consider it the most successful job-search strategy available. In fact, the weight of evidence suggests that over half the people who switch jobs find their new employers through networking. All the other job-search strategies (employment agencies, search firms, targeted and mass mailings, electronic networking, and opportunity advertisements) combined account for fewer positions than networking.

Guidelines

Networking is an art form rather than a science. Here are several guidelines that can help you get started in the right direction:

- Be careful not to wear out welcome mats with friends, associates, and other contacts. Schedule and pace your calls with thought and tact.
- Plan each call in detail: Write down your questions and any favors you may wish to ask. Limit these during a single call to what you would find reasonable if you were being called, and then reduce them even further.
- Be up front about the purpose of the call. No matter how hard you attempt to mask your true intent in chitchat, they will know when you eventually get to the point, and they may resent the waste of time and deception.
- Express an interest in the person you are calling, and be sensitive to their desire to talk about things aside from the purpose of your call.
- Pay careful attention, especially if they express opinions or offer advice. You do not have to follow their advice, but avoid arguing or expressing strong disagreement with them. You called them to ask for help, and you owe them the courtesy of listening to what they say.
- If you are able to arrange so much as an informal interview with a decision maker, do your homework to discover which of their needs you may be qualified to fill. Be prepared to ask intelligent and purposeful questions. Take notes, for all the obvious reasons.
- Say "Thank you" at the end of the conversation . . . courtesy is still in style.

Definition

What is networking? Consider the following definition:

A planned process of gathering and sharing information, ideas, and strategies through agenda-driven contacts with selected individuals in order to expand your universe of knowledge and create an awareness of your capabilities and availability.

Let's look at this more closely, element by element.

"... a planned process ..."

Here are recognizable steps to networking that bring about the results you wish to achieve. The process is planned in that you need to think through and design, in advance, the approach and words to use, and that you must identify the people you need to contact in order to maximize your success.

"... gathering and sharing information, ideas, and strategies through agenda-driven contacts ..."

As Mark Twain noted, "Reading thirty books on any one subject would cause the reader to be an expert on that subject in the eyes of most people." Networking is based upon a similar premise: Talking to a number of people who have experience and perspective in a field can dramatically increase your knowledge and perspective in that field. Planning upfront which questions and issues to raise creates your agenda. Note that the term *sharing* is also significant. When you become a resource of information and contacts for others, they will be willing to go out of their way to help you.

"... with selected individuals in order to expand your universe of knowledge ..."

The people with whom you choose to network depend on the area of knowledge to which you want and need access. You may need to develop strategies for gaining entry to a particular career field or occupational specialty. If so, you are advised to conduct your agenda-driven discussions with people who have an overall perspective on that field.

Example 1

A recent mechanical engineering graduate is looking for a position in computer-aided design (CAD). Her networking targets might be the following:

- Recent graduates who have made a transition into CAD
- Engineers who are using CAD

- Software engineers who design CAD software
- CAD instructors
- Writers, editors, and journalists in the CAD field

Example 2

An outplaced corporate manager who wants to purchase his own business feels that a franchise opportunity might be his best course of action. He should consider networking with these people:

- Current franchise owners, to determine not only their satisfaction with this form of business ownership but also their satisfaction with the product or service the franchise provides
- Business brokers who buy and sell companies
- Customers, suppliers, and competitors of the particular franchise he is interested in buying
- Business and economic writers who have studied, researched, or written about franchise ownership

". . . create an awareness of your capabilities and availability . . ."

Behaving responsibly as a person who conducts a carefully planned and agenda-driven networking program will earn you the friendship and respect of potential peers. Who better to form alliances with than people in your field of interest? Even if you simply develop a friendly relationship with your first contacts, your time is not wasted. Often, some of the best results from networking meetings come later. The business owner with whom you met may pass your name on to a friend, supplier, or consultant. The more people you impress with your planned approach, the more opportunities you are likely to evoke. The universe can open up for those who ask, politely.

Asking the Right Questions

Here's a short list of generic questions you can use to develop your own toolbox:

- What caused you to enter this field, industry, or business?
- What were your major considerations before entering this business? (Examples may include supply vs. demand, changing technologies, changing consumer dynamics, potential earning power, training, or upgrading of skills.)
- Knowing what you know now, would you enter this field today?
- Based on what you know about me (this is where your resume comes

into play), do you believe I have the necessary strengths and background to enter (advance in) this field?

- Does my resume suggest enough experience to allow me to be considered seriously for this field, industry, or business?
- If so, what might I add to improve my chances for success?
- If not, what should I add or change?
- Is there anything you would recommend I should do in order to prepare to move into this field?
- Are there any strategies I might consider to learn more about this field?
- Are there any other people you think I should contact for additional perspectives on what I'm trying to do?
- May I follow up with you at some later date to inform you of my progress?
- Is there any information that I could look for that might be helpful to you?

Avoiding the Wrong Questions

There are also pitfalls to be wary of that can destroy the most carefully laid networking plans. Avoid:

- Criticizing a third party. Your networking partner will consider that you may do the same to him or her.
- Overstaying your welcome. Stick to a time limit. "I promised to limit our meeting to thirty minutes, and I intend to keep my word." The only time it is okay to overstay your visit is when the other person suggests it.
- Arriving too early or too late. Always plan to arrive for the meeting with four or five minutes to spare. Earlier than that is boorish and shows bad time management; arriving late is disrespectful and inconsiderate.
- Taking notes without asking for permission. Always ask—most people don't mind when asked.
- Failing to summarize the ideas, suggestions, and other names given to you. This is the sign of a bad listener and calls into question your respect for the value of ideas given to you.
- Asking for a job in a networking meeting. This faux pas means instant loss of credibility and can be offensive to your partner. If you are offered a job (or opportunity to interview), you gain respect by politely deferring it to another time, for instance, "I didn't come to this meeting today with the intention of asking for an interview, although I certainly appreciate your interest. I would very much like to follow up with this opportunity as soon as might be convenient for you. Thank you."

Remember to thank the other person for his or her time, interest and effort.

By Letter, Phone or E-Mail?

Follow-ups can be conducted via (e- or snail-) mail or phone; fax and personal visits are not recommended unless specifically invited. (See Chapter 14 for details.)

Unless otherwise requested or promised, phone calls may be an imposition and can lead to awkwardness in the following cases:

- The person you call does not remember you or has nothing to tell you.
- The person is too busy to speak with you.
- You cannot reach the person and have to leave a message.

E-mail is the recommended medium for follow-ups. Your message may be informal, arrives instantly, and it can be answered at the other person's convenience.

In Summary

Networking takes practice. Your best bet is to begin with existing contacts who know you and may be more forgiving. However, make sure that these meetings do not turn into "old times" conversations from which you derive little value. When you initiate a new contact, communicate your purpose clearly. Whether you were referred by a friend or associate, or found the person's name in a journal article or directory of some kind, identify the source of the referral and then ask for an appointment of specified duration (no more than half an hour). Tell them enough about you to enable them to decide if they are willing to meet you. Be polite and brief.

One final suggestion that works wonders is to do your homework. Prior to scheduling your meetings, spend a few hours at the library to research at least a dozen articles of general appeal dealing with upbeat topics, solutions, and ideas that your future networking partners may find useful. These resources, which might cover technology, economics, human behavior, costs savings, customer service, and similar issues, enable you to produce timely and interesting references during your networking meetings. Imagine being able to pull out a relevant article and say, "In preparation for this meeting, I was thinking about how I might repay you for your time and generosity. By chance, I ran across this article that might possibly offer you a useful thought or idea."

JOAN A. COWEN
1234 Park Drive
Troy, Michigan 48084
(313) 689-5432

January 21, 2007

Mr. Jack Montgomery
Divisional Vice President
Armature Industries, Inc.
2777 Lapeer Road
Rochester Falls, MI 48091

Dear Mr. Montgomery:

Loren McMasters encouraged me to contact you because of the significant involvement you have had in strategic planning. Your comprehensive ability in assembling corporate resources into a coherent plan is very important to me.

I very recently left a strategic planning position at Kalco, Inc. As you know, Kalco, Inc., has de-emphasized centralized strategic planning by pushing it into the line. As a result, I was given the opportunity to leave voluntarily. This led me to conclude that I would have more to contribute at a higher level in an organization that values centralized planning.

May I reassure you that I am not asking you for an interview, nor do I expect that you may know of an appropriate opening. Rather, my interest is to gain your perspectives and ideas on issues that may make a difference to me. Your thoughts on companies I might target would be helpful. Additionally, any contacts you may have that might offer additional perspectives would be greatly appreciated.

Enclosed is my resume by way of offering you a picture of my background. Loren mentioned that you wrote the book on strategic planning, and I look forward to meeting you and gaining your perspectives.

Allow me to contact you in the next few days to determine when it might be convenient for us to meet.

Sincerely,

Joan A. Cowen

Cyrus Switcher
1000 Petershaw Road
Marietta, GA 30066
404/026-1000

February 7, 2007

Ms. Charlene Cerlot
1000 Clark Street
Montreal H2 x252
Quebec, Canada

Dear Charlene,

Our mutual friend, Greg Caton, encouraged me to contact you. He felt that your thoughts on the career move you made from public accounting to general management might help me in the transition I am contemplating.

It would be helpful to hear what opportunities and obstacles you faced when making this transition. How you overcame the perception of "once an accountant, always an accountant" would be of particular interest.

I have known for several years that I need a broader challenge of general management in heading up a small to mid-sized company or division. Did you move into general management for this same reason?

Charlene, I am not contacting you in the expectation that you might hire me or know where a job for me currently exists. Frankly, it is your personal experience in successfully re-applying your skills in which I am particularly interested.

Allow me to call you in the next few days and see if there is a convenient time we might discuss this further. I look forward to speaking with you.

Sincerely yours,

Cyrus Switcher

CHAPTER NINE
Advice for Job Seekers

Not even a perfect resume will land the perfect job if it is not used as part of a well-targeted and effectively conducted job search. This chapter offers advice on several topics that every job seeker should consider before sending off a single resume.

Hot Opportunities

Reporting on popular market and career opportunities is best left for Web sites and journals published on a daily, weekly, or even monthly basis. By the time a book is published, some hot areas cool and others start to simmer. No one knows for sure what the future job market holds in store, but there are ways to prepare for even this uncertainty.

Industries

Certain industries and jobs will continue to exist in some form or another; people will always need nourishment, a place to live, health care, basic services, and so on. Certain banks, brokerage houses, transportation, telecommunications, and other major industries are likely to survive the ravages of time and recession although changes will occur to their business practices and personnel requirements.

Skills

Basic communications, interpersonal, and management skills will not go out of style any time soon. Computer literacy is a necessary and transferable asset throughout the civilized world and elsewhere. A general knowledge of the industries in which you may be interested is easily obtainable on the Web and in libraries.

Attitude

An open mind, ability to recognize and adjust to change, and a willingness to learn new things and new ways to do old things are your best protection from prolonged unemployment or enforced retirement. Since you can't do anything about unemployment rates and the economy, don't worry about these issues and try to maintain a positive attitude. Take care of the small things, and the big picture will take care of itself.

Advice

Career consultants, employment agencies, executive recruiters, and human resources professionals are equipped to provide up-to-date direction and advice on the latest trends and opportunities. Don't hesitate to ask.

Foreign Jobs

Most of us should realistically limit foreign job searches to places where we speak the local language fluently. However, a uniquely desirable and recognized talent may get you invited to places where you don't need to speak their language.

In fact, the world is changing in ways unimagined only a decade ago. Outsourced information technology and services are opening doors to North Americans in India; increasing numbers of Chinese Americans are finding employment back on the Chinese mainland; and many bilingual Spanish speaking natives have discovered unique career opportunities throughout the Americas.

The majority of foreign openings available to English-only speakers are in the sciences (research and development), technology (petroleum and communications), and education (teaching), and for international agencies such as the United Nations. American and Canadian companies looking for people to work offshore are still American and Canadian companies.

Caution: Foreign countries have diverse cultures and customs that differ not only from those in the United States but also from one another. For this reason you should consult someone who has knowledge and experience of the place in question before preparing and sending off your resume. They may expect your CV (Curricula Vitae) in hard copy, e-mail, or handwritten; more or less detail about your job experience; and the kind of personal information that might be considered inappropriate at home.

Bonne chance!

Mistakes to Avoid

You might be surprised at how many irrelevant and otherwise inappropriate references are known to find their way into resumes and cover letters, which then find their way into trash bins.

Here are some rules of thumb:

- Avoid profanity and attempts at humor. We are not entirely sure if people who write the word Yes beneath Education are trying to be cute or are simply ignorant, but it happens over and again.
- Avoid personal preferences and idiosyncrasies, such as political

affinities, preferred television programs, favorite vacation sites, and the like. Year after year, misguided folk continue to make these seemingly obvious mistakes.

- Avoid criticisms of past employers. What you say about others reveals far more about you.
- Avoid lies, gross exaggerations, inappropriate keywords, and statements that stretch credibility. Assume that nearly everyone who reads your resume is an experienced professional capable of separating fact from fantasy. Take for granted that they will get a background check on you to verify the information in your resume.
- Avoid abbreviations, acronyms, and at all cost, errors. Get your resume proofed by someone reliable before you send it out.
- Avoid the impression of arrogance, excessive humility, and other annoying traits.
- Avoid lengthy, wordy, difficult-to-read-and-understand tendencies and formats. Resumes are neither experimental projects nor full-length biographies.

Unless you are looking for a job in the creative arts, avoid fancy, artsy, and generally unconventional fonts and paper. The people you want to read your resume won't bother if they have to strain their eyes. Use at least ten- to twelve-point type and choose between Arial, Courier, Times New Roman, or something similar.

Salary Considerations

Be aware of market conditions both in general and particularly in your line of work. In a buyer's market, salaries may be lower than what you are accustomed to. If your skills are rare and in demand, you may well positioned to bargain for a premium rate.

The bottom line is to be realistic. Find out what others in your field, with comparable expertise and experience to yours, are earning, and set your sights accordingly.

Timing, demand, and location are important factors in determining salary levels. A company with dozens of inexpensive, foreign workers may find your salary requirements excessive. On the other hand, if you are moving from Topeka or Bismarck to New York City or Silicon Valley, you will need to raise your expectations in accordance with a higher cost of living.

CHAPTER TEN
Cover Letters

Now that your resume has been shaped into a polished gem, it's time to focus on your cover letter. This is the tool that lends your resume direction and appeal.

A cover letter is used to introduce an enclosed resume. You may be sending it to someone who has asked to see it or initiating a contact with a placement or consulting agency. You may be targeting a specific company or individual or responding to an advertisement. Whatever the purpose, the person who receives your resume expects the courtesy and direction provided by a clear and purposeful cover letter.

Objectives

A well-written cover letter meets the following objectives:

- It offers you an opportunity to personalize and target your resume to a particular reader.
  - This is critical, since resumes are impersonal. Without a personalized cover letter, a resume may create the impression that the addressee is simply part of a mass mailing.
  - Address your cover letter to a specific individual in the target organization, preferably someone with decision-making authority. Most libraries provide resources like trade journals and directories. The company's Web site may also be helpful. If you aren't sure about who's who, call the company to verify your target's name and title. And make sure you spell the person's name correctly.
- It allows you to direct attention to specific skills and experience.
  - The primary question you need to answer to a potential employer is, "What can you do for us?" Your cover letter provides the opportunity to highlight certain skills and accomplishments that may have particular meaning to your target. You can demonstrate that you have researched the company and effectively tell them, "Here I am, the candidate you've been looking for."
- It enables you to clearly state why you are interested in the target organization.
  - This is the flip side of the preceding objective: the reasons you

are interested in the target company. Earlier you highlighted specific skills; now you suggest where they could be put to use. Once again you reinforce the image of being knowledgeable and industry-wise.

- It opens the door for further communication and follow-through.
  - The ending of your cover letter is where you can initiate the exchange of further communication, such as e-mail or a phone call.

Writing an effective cover letter is too often underestimated in the process of seeking a new job. We will contrast both *how* and *how not* to do it.

February 18, 2007

Ann Carmichael
(417) 555-4414
AnnC@overview.com

100 Valley View Terrace
Santa Fe, NM 80801

Arthur C. Reese
President
Southwest Tooling Research, Inc.
200 Mountain View Road
Santa Fe, NM 80801

Dear Mr. Reese,   LIFELESS OPENING.

Enclosed please find my resume. After you review it, I am sure you will find that
I'm a worthwhile and capable professional engineer who deserves further attention.
ESSENTIALLY, SHE IS WRITING BECAUSE SHE NEEDS A NEW JOB.
My current situation no longer offers me sufficient challenges and responsibilities.
Because of this, I feel it is time to seek out another opportunity.

If there is any interest in my capabilities, you can reach me at (417) 555-4414. I'm
positive you will find the time you spend analyzing my capabilities well worth your
time.   UNAPPEALING CLOSING.

Sincerely,

Ann Carmichael

This letter fails to include vital information, lacks a clear purpose, and does
little to entice the reader to read more. Would you bother to read the resume
attached to this cover letter if you had a stack of resumes (in addition to other
pressing documents) on your desk?

An effective cover letter (see following) conveys a sense of purpose and
enthusiasm. It should also demonstrate the writer's awareness of the target
company's goals.

February 18, 2007

Ann Carmichael
100 Valley View Terrace
Santa Fe, NM 80801

(417) 555-4414
AnnC@overview.com

Arthur C. Reese
President
Southwest Tooling Research, Inc.
200 Mountain View Road
Santa Fe, NM 80801

Dear Mr. Reese,

I read with great interest a recent article in *Engineering Today* entitled, "Southwest Tooling's Push to Maintain Engineering Excellence." Your plans to increase your Engineering Lab Team appears to be a positive sign of Southwest's continuing dedication to quality service. DEMONSTRATES AN AWARENESS OF THE COMPANY'S ACTIVITIES AND OBJECTIVES.

I am intrigued by the team research concept you have developed. The motivating force within a research team offers each member a sense of pride and accomplishment. UPBEAT PRESENTATION.

The enclosed resume demonstrates my extensive, long-range commitment to tooling research. You will also notice my own experience working with the team research concept. It goes without saying that you are looking for the best possible people to staff your growing organization. I feel that I can offer you and Southwest Tooling substantial experience and the high degree of excellence that you need.
I look forward to meeting you to discuss your opening. I will call during the early part of next week to arrange an interview and to discuss my possible involvement with Southwest Tooling. CONFIDENT ENDING.

Sincerely,

Ann Carmichael

This version puts forth all major objectives, stressing the writer's strengths and potential value (tooling research and team experience) to the company. It answers the two important questions, "Why are you sending us your resume?" and "What value can you offer us?" Then it promises to follow up.

The overall tone is enthusiastic, informative, and confident, without being wordy or overstated.

Responding to a Blind Advertisement

April 2, 2007

Harold H. Hopeful
40 Radar Street
Norfolk, VA 23510

(757) 640-4321
Hope@$$$.com

Good Day. *CLEARLY IDENTIFIES THE AD TO WHICH HE IS RESPONDING WITH AN AGGRESSIVE OPENING STATEMENT.*

The position of Chief Financial Officer, outlined in your advertisement of April 1, 2007, matches my career interests and is strongly compatible with my skills and experience.

The fact that your company is a manufacturer and distributor in both international and domestic locations is of particular interest, since these activities appear to parallel my recent activities.

As Financial Officer of an international corporation, I have considerable experience in directing the full spectrum of accounting and financial management functions. Specifically, I have:

- Designed and directed the installation of an international data communications network for reporting sales and marketing trends and totals
- Initiated and designed data processing systems providing significant improvement in reporting accuracy, management control, and organizational productivity during a period of rapid expansion
- Directed the cash management and treasury function (including planning and investment of $152 million), as well as forecasting for four divisions and fifteen markets *SOLID PROFESSIONAL AND ACADEMIC CREDENTIALS.*

Additional accomplishments are listed in the enclosed resume.

My academic qualifications include an MBA and an undergraduate degree in finance. I have been a CPA in the Commonwealth of Virginia since 1996.

You can contact me during office hours at (757) 640-4321 or at Hope@$$$.com. I am looking forward to meeting you. *UPBEAT ENDING.*

Sincerely yours,

Harold Hopeful

Harold presents his candidacy clearly and convincingly. There isn't much to criticize with this letter.

February 9, 2007

Betty B. Goode
18000 Cowan Avenue
Irvine, CA 92614

(949) 660-9999
BBG@auld.com

Dear Sir/Madam,

PROVOCATIVE OPENING STATEMENT.

I am personally responsible for $256 million worth of business in five top consumer and industrial marketing accounts.

Your company is represented as one that would appreciate the special and unusual talents I offer. Do my expertise in marketing and sales, entrepreneurial spirit, and professionally assertive nature appear to fit with your objectives? DEMONSTRATING THE ABILITY TO MARKET HERSELF.

The enclosed resume itemizes my credentials as noted in my most recent performance review. My manager described me as ". . . an outstanding member of the Marketing Team who is recognized by her peers as one of the best."

THIS IS IN RESPONSE TO A REQUEST FOR COMPENSATION REQUIREMENTS.

Compensation is something I would prefer to discuss in confidence.

I am looking forward to hearing from you soon to explore any mutually beneficial opportunities.

Yours truly,

Betty Goode

CONFIDENCE AND AN AGGRESSIVE PERSONALITY ARE STRONG SALES PREREQUISITES. MIGHT AS WELL FIND OUT UP FRONT IF THESE QUALITIES WOULD BE WELCOME.

Responding to an Identified Advertisement

March 22, 2007

Armand G. Erwyn
2636 Forest Drive
Woodbridge, IL 60517

(630) 910-1234
aerwyn@illini.com

Human Resources Department
Fizzy Beverages
100 Skokie Boulevard
Skokie, IL 60077

Dear Sir/Madam,

I am responding to your advertisement for an Accounting Representative in the *Chicago Herald*, January 7, 2007. As the following comparison shows, my experience and background appear to match your stated requirements quite closely.

YOUR REQUIREMENTS
Three to five years accounting experience.

MATCHING QUALIFICATIONS TO REQUIREMENTS.

Strong communications skills.

Knowledge of accounting systems.

IF THERE IS A CONTACT NUMBER
IN THE AD, WHY NOT USE IT?

MY QUALIFICATIONS
Five years in-depth accounting experience. Achieved impressive results by reducing costs and improving inventory control. Administered five-member staff.

Proven excellence in ongoing oral and written communications with clients and staff. Developed and presented workshops.

Experienced day-to-day processing of complex accounting systems: generated input and analyzed output. Updated legacy system to provide greater operational flexibility.

I would appreciate the opportunity to discuss the position with you personally. To this end, I will call you next week to see when we can schedule a meeting.

Yours Sincerely,

Armand Erwyn

Resume enclosed.

THIS COVER LETTER SHOWS THAT CREATIVITY
AND INTELLIGENCE CAN GO HAND-IN-HAND.

January 30, 2007

Samuel S. Stats
101010 30th Street NW
(202) 298-8888
Washington, DC 20007
Sammys@bigtime.com

Ursula P. Larsson
Primebucks Recruitment, Inc.
1000 F Street NW
Washington, DC 20004

Dear Ms. Larsson,   A CREATIVE WAY TO CAPTURE THE READER'S ATTENTION.

No doubt some of your clients are facing a problem common to many sectors and industries: how can they stay competitive in a fluctuating market? Perhaps one of them is looking for a seasoned and broadly based executive seeking to continue a successful management career in the automotive components and manufacturing arena.

A sample of my successful solutions include setting in motion a quality productivity program; establishing controls on raw and in-process inventories to increate cash flow; and reducing absenteeism by implementing a point system for feedback and control. I have also improved manufacturing methods to stabilize direct and indirect labor costs-to-sale ratios in the face of labor cost increases.

SHOWCASING HIS EXTENSIVE EXPERIENCE.

Examples:

• Instituted system for in-house brazing: increased first-year profits by over $800,000 and over $2,000,000 over three years.
• Recommended acquisition of a company, leading to increased markets and profitability.
• Organized a tooling machine spin-off that increased parent company profits by 7%.

ACCOUNTABILITY AND MEASURABLE RESULTS.

Further details are included in the enclosed resume. Should my background fit one of your current client assignments, I would be pleased to discuss the possibility with you.

Sincerely,

Samuel S. Stats   AN OUT-OF-WORK EXECUTIVE LOOKING FOR A JOB. THIS LETTER MAKES IT EASY FOR THE RECRUITER TO MATCH THE APPLICANT WITH ANY APPROPRIATE OPENINGS.

May 5, 2007

Jorge Sepulveda
23 El Segundo Terrace
San Diego, CA 12345

619/222-9999
elchefe@tamale.com

> ASIDE FROM THE PERSONALIZED ADDRESS AND GREETING, THE REST OF THE LETTER IS BOILERPLATE.

Mr. Burgess Highside
The Cardboard Box Company
23 Package Place
San Diego, CA 12345

Dear Mr. Highside,

American companies need strong manufacturing leadership that inspires their employees and delivers high-quality, low-cost products on time.
I have worked hard to be that kind of leader, and my customers, suppliers, colleagues, and employees would support my claim. My record over the last twelve years shows that I have built teams, raised performance, lowered costs, and delivered quality on-time! More specifically:

•   As Plant Manager of a $60 million, 400-employee high-tech stamping operation, my group was named "Plant of the Year" by Stamping Technology Review.
•   While Manufacturing Director for solenoids and switches, I landed two of the largest customer orders in our history. Both customers placed their orders on the strength of our quality and on-time delivery record.

> MEASURABLE ACCOMPLISHMENTS.

My Bachelor's Degree in Mechanical Engineering was earned at the Ohio State University; I am currently finishing course work for the Executive Management Program at San Diego State University.

I would like an opportunity to apply my skills in a larger organization like the Cardboard Box Company. I look forward to the possibility of discussing how I might contribute to your continued success. My resume is attached for your consideration.

> LOW-KEY FOLLOW-UP SUGGESTION.

Sincerely,

Jorge (George) Sepulveda

> THE IDEA OF A MASS MAILING IS TO CAST YOUR LINE TO THE WINDS, DEPENDING ON WHERE YOU ARE WILLING TO WORK.

Be sure to keep a record of your mailing list. It is embarrassing and unprofessional to get a call from someone you wrote to and not remember who they are.

April 1, 2007

Sally O'Selly
1000 East Second Street
Scottsdale, AZ 85251

480/946-6666
SOS@hotsales.com

Fight & Switch Company
2345 North Central Avenue
Phoenix, AZ 85004

Dear Sir/Madam,   ANOTHER BOILERPLATE, BUT WITH PIZZAZZ.

The marketplace has grown more competitive than ever. New companies with new products, old companies with better products, and all with aggressive sales forces are slicing off ever-smaller portions of a dwindling pie.   WHO WOULD DISAGREE?

Perhaps you have experienced concern in recent months that your organization's sales force is not quite up to this level of competition. Or you may have wanted to enhance the capabilities of a pretty good group. Achieving either of these objectives requires strong and innovative sales management at the executive level. This is my reason for writing to you.

If you are concerned with sales performance, I invite you to take a close look at my enclosed resume. You may discover some qualities you might like to draw upon. Here is a brief overview of my accomplishments.

• Led my company to become the major supplier of polymer resins to nine of the top dozen users.
• Supervised the development of amorphous liquids to allow for deeper industry penetration (tripled sales in three years).
• Created a productive, harmonious sales force, decreasing sales costs while increasing sales results by nearly 45% over three years.   MEASURABLE RESULTS.

Please feel free to call me at the above number if you would like to arrange an interview.   LOW-KEY ENDING SOFTENS THE EARLIER TONE.

Yours truly,

Sally O'Selly

FEW MARKETING OPERATIONS ARE SATISFIED WITH THEIR SALES PERFORMANCE. SALLY USES CONFIDENCE AND HIGH ENERGY TO COMPETE IN A TRADITIONALLY MALE ENVIRONMENT.

February 18, 2007

Melvin Marvelous
100 Overland Trail   (866) 597-7777
Houston, TX 77090   Marvelocity@TTT.net

Mr. Mike Ramchip
Texas Techies, Inc.
200 Ronan Park Place
Houston, TX 77060

Dear Mr. Ramchip,

I am a senior Web developer with demonstrated skills and experience in Java, HTML, XML, Active X, ASP, JSP, and CGI. THIS LIST OF ACRONYMS IS RIGHT ON TARGET FOR A WEB DEVELOPER.

Most recently, I have developed interactive sites for the sports programs of two colleges and one professional team organization. My work has been called attention getting and thorough. The enclosed resume will provide you with a detailed list of former clients and responsibilities.

My preference is for consulting work, although I would be willing to consider an appropriate full-time position in the Houston area. FLEXIBILITY ALWAYS HELPS.

Yours,

Mel Marvelous

INFORMALITY IS COMMON TO CONSULTANTS, ESPECIALLY WHEN ADDRESSING A CONSULTING AGENCY. MEL PROVIDES A CLEAR OVERVIEW OF HIS SKILLS AND A SMOOTH INTRODUCTION TO HIS RESUME.

CHAPTER ELEVEN
Personal Promo Letters

The personal promo letter concept is too important to ignore in a comprehensive guide to writing resumes. Not to be confused with cover letters, which introduce and accompany resumes, the promo (also sales or broadcast) letter serves as a substitute for a resume. It is primarily used when writing to selected prospects rather than employment agencies, classified ads, and so on.

Since the emphasis of *The Resume Handbook* focuses on resumes, this section is offered as a brief guide to writing successful promo letters.

Purpose

The purpose of a personal promo letter is to offer an innovative alternative to sending a resume. It allows you to tailor your experience to the specifications of a position and a company. This approach can be effective when writing to a large number of corporations where you hope to attract the interest of a key decision-maker and to explore the possibility of a current or future opening. It is not intended as a response to advertisements, especially where formal resumes have been requested.

Like resumes, promo letters are intended to obtain an interview. They are well suited to exploring corporate needs that may not yet have been defined, particularly for individuals with extensive experience and skills.

General Guidelines

Always direct your letter to a specific individual, not a nameless title. Try to avoid personnel and employee relations departments, for they are primarily oriented toward existing vacancies.

Use standard business-sized stationery, preferably personalized. Type "PRIVATE AND CONFIDENTIAL" on the front of the envelope, or a secretary may open the letter and automatically pass it along to Personnel.

Do not refer to specific past or current employers, and leave out any mention of current or desired salary. Keep careful notes on all correspondence; be sure you have a quick, efficient way to locate a specific reference if someone to whom you've written calls unexpectedly.

Content

Opening Paragraph

Your opening paragraph is the attention-grabber. This is where you capture the reader's curiosity and entice him or her to continue reading. Unusual, intriguing information related to your objectives is a solid bet:

- I increased the output of my department 212% while reducing billable working hours.
- I made a successful living for seven years selling African coffee in Brazil.
- As R&D Director of a major manufacturer of electronic testing instruments, I initiated the development of four highly regarded products currently in production.
- How often does one have the opportunity to engage the services of an account executive who recently captured a $7.6 million contract from a giant competitor?
- My professor referred to my final MBA project in financial modeling (just completed) as "brilliant" and "innovative." He suggested that an organization of your prominence in the banking industry could certainly make use of an honors graduate like myself, following my graduation in June of this year.

Second Paragraph

This is where you tell the reader why you are writing to him or her. It identifies the job you're aiming for, concentrating on a specific and carefully researched objective:

- This letter is intended to explore your potential need for a bilingual petroleum engineer who is willing to relocate. If you do happen to be looking for someone with my qualifications . . .
- I am writing because I anticipated that you might have need of someone with my unusual blend of skills and experience in biomedical marketing research. Should this be the case . . .
- My purpose in contacting you directly is to inquire whether you anticipate a need for an executive recruiter with extensive contacts and experience in the magazine publishing industry. If so . . .

Third Paragraph

This paragraph is intended to create interest in what you have to offer. You can state what you have accomplished in your field or list related accomplishments that support the kind of job you're seeking. Describe outstanding achievements (from your resume) that directly support the job objective. Use short, direct sentences. Avoid boastful adjectives like *incredible* or *terrific*. Cite specific figures. Don't hesitate to say:

- I accomplished / achieved / succeeded in . . .
- I have received six patents, with eleven pending, on . . .
- I saved my company $8.2 million by reducing . . .
- As Director of Marketing of a small company, I increased sales by 67% over a period of . . .
- My architectural design was selected and implemented . . .

Fourth Paragraph

State specific, positive facts about your education and other qualifications that can be verified. Includes dates only if potentially useful to you:

- MS (with honors) in Management from the University of Michigan. I majored in Personnel Relations, and minored in Industrial Psychology.
- In 2006, I passed the tenth (final) actuarial exam for New York State.
- I authored the 120-page "Guide to XYZ Information Retrieval" (published by XYZ, Inc., 2004).

Fifth Paragraph

The final paragraph tells the addressee what action you suggest on his or her part or what may be expected from you. Let them know when and where you can be conveniently contacted:

- It would be my pleasure to offer you additional details regarding my qualifications during an interview. You can reach me most evenings and weekends at the above number. I am looking forward to hearing from you at your earliest convenience.
- I hope to hear from you prior to June 1, at which date I am expected to make a decision as to whether I will remain . . .
- I plan to be in Chicago the week of February 2–6. In the event that you would like to arrange an interview during this period, you can reach me at my home (212/123-4567) after 6:30 most evenings throughout the month of January.

Then sign the letter.

To put these principles into practice, a self-promo example letter follows. We recommend a one-page format, which is more inviting to the reader.

February 9, 2007

Carl Corral
133 Charter Boulevard
Berkley, MI 48077

(414) 555-9876
ccorral@loa.com

Mr. Ira Azimov
Vice-President, Engineering Systems
Robotics Corporation
3333 Euclid Avenue
Cleveland, OH 44114

Dear Mr. Azimov,

> AN OPENING STATEMENT THAT DEMANDS ATTENTION. MEASURABLE ACCOMPLISHMENTS INCLUDED.

In the past thirty-two months I have successfully designed, installed, and made operational a computer-controlled, visually activated robotics system. This system has already saved my firm over $875,000, with additional savings projected to more than double that amount through 2008.

I have been following your firm's robotics efforts with great interest, especially with regard to visual scanning applications. Your pioneering innovations complement my own research and have prompted me to contact you.

> SHOWS AWARENESS OF AND INTEREST IN TARGET COMPANY.

Permit me to list some personal accomplishments:

- Received the John A. Cartwright Award as 2006 "Research Engineer of the Year," Michigan Chapter.
- Published article, "Light Shading Activators in Visual Sensing Devices," Journal of Electrical Engineers, December, 2005.
- Improved on-time completion of scheduled projects by 39% during my first year as Director of Research (2000), saving nearly $300,000 in early bid placements.
- Redesigned three major assembly lines, reducing downtime by 115%, reducing scrap by 55%, and improving product quality by 35%. An independent audit firm conservatively estimated bottom-line impact of these redesigns at $4.2 million.

> ACHIEVEMENTS THAT LEND CREDIBILITY.

My MSEE was earned with honors at the University of Michigan.

> SOLID ACADEMIC CREDENTIALS.

It would be my pleasure to offer you additional details on how I might contribute to Robotics' future efforts in engineering and robotics research. Please feel free to call me any evening after 7 P.M. at home. I look forward to receiving your call.

Sincerely,

> LOW-KEY FOLLOW-UP SUGGESTION.

Carl Corral

Conclusion

These principles can be applied to virtually every profession. Personal promo letters allow you to highlight elements of your background in a more personalized format and to branch off from the more traditional approaches.

Used alone or in conjunction with some of the other approaches (such as networking and the Internet), this technique can be surprisingly effective.

CHAPTER TWELVE
Following Up

The art of follow-up is overlooked by most job-searchers and can provide a winning edge when used with tact and proper timing. Follow-ups can be conducted via e-mail, snail mail, or phone; fax and personal visits are not recommended unless invited.

There are four basic reasons for following up on an earlier contact:

1. As a simple act of courtesy to thank someone for his or her time, attention, and consideration, whether you are interested in pursuing matters with them or not.
2. To furnish additional information or documents promised or requested; in this case, not to follow up is an indication of unreliability or no further interest.
3. To confirm that you have forwarded certain materials, in case they get lost or misplaced.
4. To express strong interest and enthusiasm in a job, company, or service.

Convenience

- A one-page letter is the ideal follow-up to an initial e-mail contact. The receiver can open and read it at his or her leisure and may also appreciate the convenience of a clean and attractive copy of your resume. They are less likely to throw away hard copy than to delete an e-mail message, unless they simply have no interest in you.
- Phone calls risk annoying busy people, especially if they have someone else on hold, and they may not remember who you are without your resume in front of them. If you leave a message on their machine or with another person, they may feel obligated to return your call even if they have nothing new to tell you.
- E-mail is appropriate for the second and third reasons listed above; for the other two, it may be better than nothing.
- Faxes have a way of getting lost or damaged. Unless requested, don't.

Tact

If you are not expecting an acknowledgment, do not ask for one. State the reason for your follow-up note or call, and close with a polite phrase that does not attempt to obligate a response.

- Good: I will be pleased to hear from you if you would like any additional information or to pursue my potential candidature for the position.
- Bad: Please let me know when I should expect to hear from you.

Remember also that too much of a good thing is a bad thing. If you do not hear back from someone after an initial follow-up, wait at least two weeks before trying again. Be careful not to allow your enthusiasm to grow into an annoyance.

April 22, 2007
RHC@rhythm.com

Robert H. Crosby
772 Memorial Drive
Cambridge, MA 02139

Mr. Tom Jones
British Sound Systems, Ltd.
4000 Hanover Street
Boston, MA 02113

Dear Tom, IF A FIRST-NAME BASIS HAS BEEN ESTABLISHED, THERE IS NO REASON NOT TO CONTINUE IT.

Thank you for taking the time to meet with me yesterday.

I would like to reiterate my interest in British Sound Systems and appreciate your willingness to forward my resume to one of the decision-makers you mentioned.

Sincerely,

Bob Crosby   THIS BRIEF ACKNOWLEDGMENT SERVES TO REMIND THE TARGET OF HIS PROMISE TO PASS THE RESUME ALONG.

April 23, 2007
LyndaT@you.com

Lynda Tylor
1000 Officers Row
Vancouver, WA 98661

Ms. Agatha Kristy
Twilight Mysteries
5000 NW 334th Street
Ridgefield, WA 98660

Dear Agatha,

It was a pleasure speaking with you last week.

Your enthusiasm is infectious, and I hope I've done as well to represent myself as you did for Twilight Mysteries. ENTHUSIASM WITHOUT OBLIGATION.

The writing samples you requested are attached. I look forward to the possibility of further contact. FOLLOWING UP ON A PROMISE.

Yours sincerely,

Lynda   EACH OF THESE FOLLOW-UPS IS EQUALLY SUITED TO BOTH E-MAIL AND SNAIL MAIL.

CHAPTER THIRTEEN
Other Job-Search Methods

There are seven additional strategies that account for fewer than half of all job changes:

1. Opportunity advertisements
2. Employment agencies
3. Search firms
4. State employment agencies
5. Targeted mailings
6. Mass mailings
7. Job fairs

A well-orchestrated search is likely to apply a combination of one or more of these strategies together with networking. In our experience, the vast majority of successful job changes used networking and one or more additional strategies in tandem. Your patience, persistence, and skill in blending them together is likely to determine how long it takes you to find a new position, as well as the quality of the opportunities you uncover.

If you are employed while looking for a new job, these other strategies may be easier to place into action during nonworking hours. Their advantage is that they allow you to cover the market rather quickly and with minimal interpersonal contact.

However, the impersonal aspect presents a potential danger, that of relying solely on these strategies and neglecting networking altogether. We strongly caution you to avoid this lapse.

Strategy #1—Opportunity Advertisements

Today's job changers are prone to read the want ads less seriously than in the past. The prevailing view is that advertisements are a numbers game, with choice opportunity ads pulling hundreds of resume responses. So why bother? Perhaps for the following reasons:

- Responding to an ad requires little effort. Unless your job skills are unusually obscure, you should be able to locate and respond to several ads each week.

- Attractive opportunity ads are more plentiful than you think. The majority of searchers only check their local daily newspapers for opportunity ads. But trade publications, association newsletters, and national business publications are excellent resources. Most of the major metropolitan areas also have weekly newspapers, magazines, and Web releases that cover their local business community. A day online or at the local library can be an eye-opener for anyone looking for a job.

- This is why we urge you to read through the entire run of advertisements whenever you open the employment section. Little-known and newly relocated companies can introduce themselves to you, and interesting opportunities and potential business strategies may appear under unexpected headings.

- Not enough experience? Respond anyway! We encourage you to give any ad that interests you a shot. What does it cost you? Just a little paper, time, postage, and energy. If you match on even a few of the requested skills and experience requirements, your resume may snare some interest.

Blind Ads vs. Open Ads

Blind ads are those in which the advertiser's name is withheld. Open ads identify the name of the company and sometimes the name of their recruiter.

Blind Ads

The most common concern in responding to a blind ad is that it may involve a company where you might be embarrassed or compromised by having your name surface as a job changer. One way to negate this potential inconvenience is to *double-envelope* your response. The inside or second envelope containing your resume should be marked with the following message: "Important Note—If Box 123 represents the ABC Company, please destroy this envelope and contents unopened."

This suggestion is based on the assumption that blind ads draw mail first to a box at the newspaper. They, in turn, usually forward all resume responses to the unnamed company running the blind ad. Most newspapers will honor your request if you ask that your resume not be forwarded to a named company.

Open Ads

Try to avoid addressing yourself to the personnel or human resources department, even if this is requested. Instead, call the company named in the ad and make an effort to identify the name and title of the individual who heads the division or department where the advertised position lies.

In both cases: When responding to any ad—open or blind—do not mail a response on the first day the ad appears. Wait at least four days before you mail your response. The idea is to have your resume reach them at a time when there is less competition for their attention. Send out a second response about two weeks after the first one, adding the following note: "This letter and enclosed resume are my second response to your ad of (date). Please allow my double response to be an indication of my strong interest in your opportunity."

Note 1: Never send out an initial or second response to a blind ad later than thirty days after the date of the original ad. Newspapers will rarely forward boxed responses after thirty days.

Note 2: We do, however, encourage you to respond late to open ads—even three or four weeks after the ad first appeared. Many companies don't even begin interviewing and selecting candidates until several weeks after running an ad. The advice "Better late than never" certainly applies here.

Strategies #2 and #3—Employment Agencies and Search Firms

Employment agencies and search firms work for the folks who pay them, that is to say, their corporate clients—not for you. Do not approach them under the impression that they exist to find you a job. Their mission is not to market you but rather to locate competent individuals who match their clients' requirements. In reality, your contact with them merely adds you to the pool of people they hope to match with positions they are seeking to fill.

Which may be better for you, an employment agency or a search firm? The answer is based largely on where you fall within the organization chart.

Search firms tend to deal almost exclusively with mid-management through senior executive positions commanding minimum salaries of at least $75,000. If you fall into this range, consider sending your resume to ten or fifteen search firms that specialize in your field.

Search firms either concentrate in one field or generalize and cover several industries. They typically work on a retainer basis with a portion of their fee paid up front by the client. They may even serve as the exclusive source of candidates for a particular corporate client, acting as consultants to the company's senior management. Their reputation is built on consistently providing their clients with quality candidates.

Employment agencies may also specialize or generalize. The difference is that the majority of positions handled by employment agencies are likely to pay under $75,000, covering entry-level clerical and administrative jobs up through senior technical and mid-management openings.

Like search firms, they serve their corporate clients by finding suitable candidates; finding you a job is only a by-product. Employment agencies are paid contingent on finding suitable candidates who get hired. In contrast to search firms, they are less likely to be paid a retainer.

How to Use Search Firms and Employment Agencies

Timing is everything. Since most active agencies and firms only work on a few openings at a time, you need to match up your skills with their current opportunities. Your best bet is to get your resume out to a number of agencies or firms. Address it first to specialists in your field, and only then to generalists.

Do your homework. Identify all of the agencies and/or search firms that cover your skills and specialty. An excellent source is the Directory of Executive Recruiters (online at *www.kennedyinfo.com*).

This directory offers a comprehensive list of over 15,000 executive recruiters at 5,600 search firms. The extensive information provided on each entry should easily allow you to identify appropriate targets for your resume. Available options include Management Consultants, Executive Career Management, and Executive Recruiters.

Include salary information: Playing coy with firms and agencies just isn't smart. It's best to be open, honest, and realistic about yourself. Your targeted list of firms or agencies either can or cannot help you. By offering clear details about your skills, experience, and salary expectations, you make their job easier. Here are a few ways to address salary expectations in your cover letter (pick the one that most closely matches your situation):

- "I'm very open on salary requirements at this time, as I am much more interested in challenge, opportunity, and a chance to work within the industry (or field)."
- "I am interested in a position with a compensation package, including salary, benefits, and incentives, in the range of $75,000 to $90,000."
- "Currently, my salary is $65,000. I am most interested in opportunities in the mid $70s."
- "Although challenge, opportunity, and the reputation of the company I join are very important, please be aware that my total compensation during the last five years has placed me in the $120,000 to $140,000 range."

Identify seemingly obscure skills. Employment agencies and search firms make their reputations on uncovering needles in haystacks. They are in business to find people with unusual skill sets. So include in your cover letter any attributes, skills, and experiences that may round you off as owning a unique combination of capabilities. Languages, technical and interpersonal skills, and specific project- or client-related talents and experiences can make a difference in getting you noticed.

Communicating with Recruiters

Don't call agencies or firms after a mailing. They can only help you if you match a job they are currently working on, and your unsolicited calls will be seen as an unnecessary irritation by the recruiter. A better bet if you haven't heard from your initial mailing is to do a second mailing three to five weeks later.

Bear in mind that search firms and employment agencies are only parts of a balanced approach. Relying on these as your sole source of opportunity is naïve, limiting, and potentially futile.

Strategies #4 and #5—Targeting and Mass Mailings

Targeted mailings are as different from mass mailings as laser beams from sunlight. Targeted mailings rely on concentrated and selective preparation. They emphasize quality over quantity. Mass mailings, on the other hand, operate on the principle that more is better. Like direct-mail advertising, they play a numbers game by trying to coax a response with a large-scale and relatively undiscriminating approach. Only by understanding this distinction can you hope to maximize their advantages. Let's start with targeted mailings.

Targeted Mailings

Meticulous research is required to identify people and organizations that might be interested in your unique combination of abilities. The more thorough your research, the more likely you are to identify the right target companies.

Introduce yourself to your local librarian. Be explicit about what you're trying to accomplish. Most well-stocked libraries have a wealth of references and directories you will find helpful. Some of the better-known directories include the following:

Dun's Million Dollar Database (*www.dnbmdd.com/mddi*): This directory offers information on about 1,600,000 U.S. and Canadian leading public and private businesses, including industry information with size criteria (employees and annual sales), type of ownership, principal executives, and biographies.

Mergent Online (*www.mergentonline.com*): An Internet-accessible subscription service covering 10,000 public companies and their SEC filings. International company data includes more companies from more countries than any other international database, with global searching across databases.

ThomasNet (*www.thomasnet.com*): A comprehensive online resource for finding companies and products.

Federation of International Trade Associations (*www.fita.org*).

Union of International Associations (*www.uia.org*).

Dialog (*www.dialog.com*).

This is just the tip of the iceberg, but it will introduce you to the many excellent sources available at your local, college, or university library. Remember, the better your research, the better your targeted mailings. In this day and age of niche marketing, we need all the help we can get.

In summary, quality research can lead you to companies, people, associations that are closely aligned with your skills and career goals. The extent to which you are able to pinpoint quality targets for your mailings dramatically increases your likelihood of receiving quality responses.

Mass Mailings

A well-executed job search may result in fifty to possibly hundreds of mass mailings.

Mass mailings require less research, but due to the numbers involved they can result in positive dividends. Based on volume alone, mass mailings are best used by job seekers with broad skills in less specialized occupations.

Middle-level managers might consider doing a mass mailing, for example, to all manufacturing companies within their region or up to a certain distance from their home. Controllers or accounting managers could conceivably work anywhere their types of skills may be in demand. College seniors starting out on the job trail with an interest in sales and marketing could mass mail their resumes to the *Fortune* 1000. The objective here is to cover the market like a blanket.

Follow these steps to conduct a mass mailing of your resume.

Obtain a Mailing List

You can develop your own, which is time consuming (but less costly), or you buy one from a mailing-list company. Purchasing a mailing list can be very cost-effective in the medium and long run. Here are few available sources:

E-Mail Results.com (*www.copywriter.com/lists/*)
Polk (*company.monster.com/polk*)
Job.com
Monster.com
USAJobs.opm.gov
Sun.com
employmentguide.com

When buying or using an existing mailing list, make sure it has been recently updated (within the past month), and that it contains the names and titles of the individuals who head up the company function appropriate to your skills and job-search goal.

Use Proper Address

Address your mailings to a specific individual whose title and responsibility appear to match your search objective. For example, if you are a sales and marketing candidate, direct your letters to the Chief Sales and/or Marketing

Executive; if you are an engineer, send yours to the Head of Engineering or Manufacturing. Focus on finding the best targets for your mailing. Never mass mail to the human resources or personnel departments—unless you want to work in personnel or human resources.

Go for Broad Appeal

Write your cover letter to appeal to the largest number of employers possible, as in the mass mailing examples on page 141 (Cover Letter #6) and 142 (Cover Letter #7). Remember to maintain a record of your mailing list and to keep it close to hand for quick and easy reference.

CHAPTER FOURTEEN
Trends

Business trends are different from those in clothes and entertainment in that they tend to fit into a logical and predictable pattern. Unlike the latest sneakers, resumes are not intended to be hip—unless you happen to work in fashion design, advertising, or a related field. In most areas, resumes need primarily to be relevant.

The majority of changes and innovations affecting resumes over the past decade stem from the Internet. Designing search-friendly resumes and posting them successfully are the latest meaningful trends. Let's focus on how to accomplish these objectives.

Advice

The Internet itself is full of trendy advice as to what is hot and what is not. Some sites appear to have recently discovered that vaguely stated objectives and statements like "References on Request" are out of vogue. The Resume Handbook has identified these mistakes since the very first edition, many years before the desktop computer revolution took hold, and continues to offer practical, commonsense suggestions. As seen elsewhere in this book, properly worded objectives can be effective in attracting attention to the body of a resume.

Companies that hire large numbers of employees tend to use their own Web sites and (particularly niche) job boards to review resumes. Commercial resume databases also draw their share of attention. Again, the Internet is packed with references, directions, and offers of free postings. There are also books available for anyone dedicated to studying the subject. For those to whom time may be more precious, we have done our best to summarize and encapsulate the essence of this information into a few meaningful paragraphs.

E-Resumes

An electronic resume, in whatever format, is submitted via e-mail to a company site, a job board, or a personal Web page. Ideally, this design should enable the resume to be included in a database that can be searched by keywords (discussed later in this chapter). Some sites and job boards actually specify how this should be done, such as by removing certain types of formatting. Others may request that you enter your information field by field into their formatted site.

What's the difference between a keyword-searchable e-resume and one you attach in a Word file format? Mainly formatting, since resumes created in a word processor may not perfectly accommodate a searchable database. The simplest way to deal with this issue is to cut and paste your word-processed resume into the body of the e-mail message, taking care to fix any of the formatting that gets messed up in the process.

If you aren't sure which way your target audience might prefer to receive your resume, you can include one version in the e-mail message, as above, and your original, formatted version (in MS Word or another file format) as an attachment. That covers you in both directions. Be sure to specify in the message which formats you are providing.

Text-Based

The easiest way to create a text-based e-resume is to take these steps:

- Save it (in the word-processor software) in .txt format.
- Reopen it in a text editor program (WordPad, Notepad, or Simple Text).
- Edit it as needed.

Remember, the text-based e-resume may not look as good as the formatted version, but its primary objective is to be searchable by keywords.

Scan-ability

Check each company's Web site to see if they list their own guidelines for submitting text-based, scan-able resumes. Otherwise, use the following guidelines:

- Write your name at the top of every page.
- Left justify your text, and stay within the range of 10 to 14 point type size.
- Avoid fancy fonts (we advise this for all resumes)—stick to Arial, Helvetica, Courier, Times, or something similar.
- Caps are okay, but underlining, bold, italics, graphics, shading, bullets, and symbols are taboo.
- Use standard (8½ x 11) white paper and print on a laser or high-quality inkjet (not dot matrix) printer.
- Make sure the copy you send is clear and nonsmudged, and mail it unfolded in an appropriate envelope. Folds, staples, and faxed copies may detract from the quality of the scan.

Posting

The Web is loaded with venues offering to post your e-resume. How many of these should you use? It's best to be discriminating. After all, the more places your resume appears, the more likely it is that your current employer may discover it.

Monster.com, QuintCareers.com, Jobs.AOL.com, and Hotjobs.com are among the dozens of available resume-posting services. Recruiting sources tend to be more focused (such as by state or for government jobs). To narrow your selection, search for sites that focus on your area of expertise and interest.

If you want to set up your own Web site, companies like AddPro.com, Blast Engine (*www.blastengine.com*), and Submission Pro (*www.submissionpro.com*) (to name a few) offer reasonably priced search engine submission and registration services.

Keep track of each and every Web posting service that you use. Revisit them at least monthly to be sure your resumes are still active and that no errors or deletions have damaged them.

Keywords

As mentioned earlier, keywords are essential to database searches because that's where many resumes end up—in databases that can be searched by keywords. In an e-resume, a list of up to twenty keywords may be acceptable, as long as they are relevant to the work you seek and the experience described in the body of your resume. But exercise restraint; overuse of keywords begins to look like spam.

We have mixed feelings about including keyword lists in traditional resumes, since these terms are better represented within the context of job histories and education. Describing how and where you used or acquired certain skills and familiarity with various applications is more convincing than simply listing them.

Afterword

The glut of materials available on common subjects bears testament to the saying that there's more than one path to a given destination. Of course, some roads are more efficient and direct than others. When it comes to providing information on topics like resumes and cover letters, a reference that provides you with a few clear strategies and practical suggestions can be well worth your time.

In poker and the job market, as elsewhere in life, luck plays a significant role in determining where we find ourselves at any given time. Nevertheless, a rational game plan based on solid information and experience is more likely to minimize the random factors and reduce an arbitrary flow of unexpected circumstance.

The guidelines and suggestions in *The Resume Handbook* are geared toward enabling control over the factors that govern one specific goal: getting the interviews you want! To this end we have introduced you to the ingredients of a number of successful resumes with realistic examples and commentaries. By now you recognize all of the following:

- Relevant vs. useless information
- Topics to avoid
- Active vs. static
- Attention-grabbing vs. bland and unappealing
- Cover letters vs. personal sales letters

You now know how to handle these important things:

- Emphasize strengths and de-emphasize weaknesses
- Focus on (career vs. immediate) objectives
- Write an interview-winning resume

Poor resumes close more doors than the mischievous winds of fortune. Effective resumes, based on purpose and technique, are universally recognized throughout the business world. *The Resume Handbook* can help you to develop an effective strategy designed to get your foot inside the door.

The rest is up to you!